MW01640262

MLS
MLS

fuji
FUJIFILM
adidas
adidas
adidas

AIG
CONRAD
12
23
9

HARRINGTON
2
AIG

For the
BESLER
5
SINOVIC
16
ESPINOZA
15
MYERS
7

of the City
OLUM
CESAR
55
6
CUP FINAL

CAULDRON
FIGHT LIKE HELL

ONE CLUB

THE FIRST 25 YEARS OF MAJOR LEAGUE SOCCER IN KANSAS CITY

Pages 2-3: The famous "Digital Crawl" celebration, circa 1996. From left to right, Mark Chung, goalscorer Digital Takawira, and Diego Gutierrez.

Pages 4-5: Jimmy Conrad (12), Roger Espinoza (17), Kei Kamara (23), Teal Bunbury (9), and Michael Harrington (2), celebrate Davy Arnaud's (center, 22) goal to open the scoring in the Wizards shock win against international giants Manchester United, July 25, 2010, while fans in the stands – many of them wearing Manchester United gear – cheer on.

Pages 6-7: Sporting's starting XI walks to the north end of the stadium, the Cauldron end, prior to the 2012 U.S. Open Cup Final against the Seattle Sounders, Aug. 8, 2012, the club's first trophy in the Sporting era.. From left to right: Matt Besler (5), Seth Sinovic (16), Roger Espinoza (15), Teal Bunbury (9), Kei Kamara (23), Chance Myers (7), Jimmy Nielsen (1), Graham Zusi (8), Lawrence Olum (13), Júlio César (55) and Paulo Nagamura (6).

Page 8: Graham Zusi takes a corner kick during a game against the Houston Dynamo, Nov., 2011.

Sporting Kansas City
2020 Baltimore Ave., 4th Floor, Kansas City, Missouri 64108

www.SportingKC.com

Sporting Kansas City is owned by:
The Patterson Family
The Illig Family
The Curran Family
The Maday Family
The Heineman Family

1 2 3 4 5 6 7 8 9 TEN 11 1 6 12 17 5 10 16

ISBN: 978-0-578-86049-7

Library of Congress Control Number: 2021905194

INTRODUCTION
BY JAKE REID PRESIDENT & CEO, SPORTING KC

In sports nothing is accomplished without a great team. We raise trophies together, and we taste defeat together. It is the hard work of every individual fulfilling their role that allows a team to experience success. As for the book you're reading right now, many people contributed to make it truly special. However, I would be remiss if I did not single out a few key individuals who poured their time and energy into this project. Their commitment to creating a book that lives up to the Sporting Way is appreciated and continues to make me extremely proud of everyone who is part of this organization.

First, a huge thank you to our ownership team. The individuals and families who comprise our ownership prefer to highlight the people at Sporting and not take any credit. However, none of us would be able to do what we do without their continued support. Their passion for Kansas City and this club always shines bright. They have made those of us who work here feel like part of a family, not part of an organization, and for that we are forever grateful.

The associates who turned this book from idea into reality deserve a lap around the pitch being applauded by everyone who reads it. As if their day jobs didn't keep them busy enough, they spent every available minute during late nights and weekends to make this happen. Chad Reynolds, Kurt Austin, Cortney Park, Rob Thomson, Sam Kovzan and Carter Augustine brought this project to life. They have been with the organization for a combined 55 years. Some lived through the rebrand, some the opening of the stadium, but all have a love for this club and what it represents to our community.

Most importantly, thank you to all of the fans. For some of you, this will be a walk down memory lane to the early Wizards years. For others, you may remember the first match at Children's Mercy Park that started your fandom. Regardless of when you began your own personal journey with us, we thank you for your passion and dedication and for making Sporting Kansas City one of the most successful clubs in the first 25 years of Major League Soccer.

With such a successful history, we are all proud of where we have been and what we have done together. As we reflect on the first quarter century, it is hard not to look ahead to the future and ponder how the next chapter will unfold. With the 2026 World Cup coming to North America, we know the future of this beautiful game is bright. We hope to raise many more trophies over the next 25 years with all of you by our side. What we all know for certain is that we will continue to represent Kansas City and strive to make every one of you proud along the way.

Opposite: Detail from display ad in March 31, 2011, Kansas City Star highlighting the club's new identity and stadium for the 2011 season.

FOREWORD

BY DON GARBER

COMMISSIONER, MLS

"I Believe That We Will Win!"

For the faithful in the Cauldron match after match, that chant never fails to bring chills.

And rightfully so. I remember hearing it for the first time and thinking, "this is going to become a rallying cry not only for Sporting Kansas City, but for the entire sport of soccer in America." And every time I hear the roar of the supporters when I'm at a game in Kansas City, I think, "they have every reason to believe." After all, Sporting Kansas City fans have been first-hand witnesses to one of the greatest turnaround stories in the sports industry during the modern era.

Anyone who follows Major League Soccer or the business of sports knows this is not hyperbole. When I'm asked to name some of the most important achievements in the first quarter-century of the league's history, the rebirth of Sporting Kansas City and revival of MLS in this community is always at the top of the list. This club is living proof that with committed and passionate local ownership, a world-class stadium, a terrific fan experience, talented players and a sharp technical staff, any team in MLS can achieve a similar level of success.

I'm glad *One Club* has been published to serve as a historical document of the first 25 years of the club. It begins with the birth of the Kansas City Wiz thanks to Lamar Hunt, one of the most visionary owners in professional sports and one of the founders of Major League Soccer. Lamar loved the game, and his belief in a limitless future for a major professional soccer league in America was a driving force in the creation of our league. It was Lamar who insisted that a major league city like Kansas City needed to be home to a Major League Soccer club.

Without Lamar's vision and leadership, Kansas City would not have been one of the charter MLS teams when the league launched in 1996, and the Wizards would not have won their first MLS Cup four years later. The efforts of the Hunt family for soccer in the city and across the U.S. will be remembered forever, as will the on-field heroics of your favorite stars of the Wizards era, such as Preki, Tony Meola, Mo Johnston, Chris Klein, Digital Takawira, Jimmy Conrad, and a future manager and sporting director named Peter Vermes. In my early years as commissioner, the Wizards made history when they rose from last place in the Western Conference in 1999 to capture both MLS Cup and the Supporters' Shield in 2000 under head coach Bob Gansler.

However, by 2004, the future of MLS in Kansas City was uncertain. The Hunts owned multiple MLS clubs and wanted to focus on only one, and for them it was their team in Dallas—the longtime family home. Attendance in Kansas City was down and interest from fans and local businesses had decreased. Unless the league found strong local ownership, we wondered if we could survive in Kansas City.

The league and Lamar believed the club needed dedicated owners with roots in the city, a passion for the game and a willingness to be innovative. At the time, I honestly did not know if we would be able to find a local owner who believed in the sport and had the vision to see how soccer can help inspire and motivate not only the city, but the entire region.

That changed when Lamar met with Cliff Illig and Neal Patterson, two of Kansas City's most respected business leaders and community supporters. Joining Cliff were several other local owners —Greg Maday, Pat Curran and Robb Heineman—who together worked to not only keep the team in the city, but change the course of soccer in the Midwest.

The transition to new ownership set in motion the revival of the organization, beginning with a new brand—Sporting Kansas City—that reflected a culture shift that would expand beyond the team and include a deep connection with fans and the community. The new ownership group developed a new business model, built on data analytics with a focus on truly understanding the needs of every soccer fan as well as corporate and media partners.

The technical staff—led by Peter Vermes, an

of the National Soccer Hall of Fame—built a winning culture and developed a player development system from youth to the USL and the first team.

And, of course, there was the opening of a world-class soccer stadium delivering an unrivaled fan experience.

When what is now known as Children's Mercy Park opened in 2011, it immediately became one of the great soccer stadiums of its size in the world. The design was dramatic. The supporters' section and other fan amenities created an unparalleled experience for every attendee. Not long after they played in a cavernous NFL stadium and a minor league baseball stadium, Sporting had a sellout streak of 125 matches at the new venue.

A decade later, the stadium remains one of the crown jewels of MLS due to the club's innovative and technologically advanced approach. The club and their stadium are an industry leader in customer service, ticketing solutions, gameday merchandising, food and beverage, and in-game fan engagement.

The unique and exciting fan experience has positioned Children's Mercy Park as a "go to" stadium for the United States men's and women's national teams, the Concacaf Gold Cup, international soccer matches and many MLS special events.

And Sporting KC isn't resting on their laurels. In 2018, the club opened the Compass Minerals National Performance Center, a state-of-the-art training facility for Sporting's first team as well as the home for U.S. Soccer's national coaching education. It's this kind of investment—not only in the present, but also solidifying the future—that shows what our clubs and league truly can aspire to be.

Since the club was rejuvenated by local ownership, MLS has grown from 12 teams in 2006 to 27 in 2021 with more clubs to come. Needless to say, when a league is trying to grow, it helps to have an incredible model like Sporting Kanas City as a prime example of what soccer in North America can be. When you add the significant involvement of Cliff Illig, and his son, Michael, to countless MLS committees, every potential MLS investor visits Kansas City to see their stadium, training facility, and most importantly, learn about their ingredients to success.

Of course, what matters most is winning, and Sporting has won its share of trophies over the last decade—MLS Cup in 2013, and U.S. Open Cups in 2012, 2015 and 2017. In 2020, they had the best year-over-year improvement in the Supporters' Shield standings in MLS history, rising from 22nd place in 2019 to third place in a year filled with challenges during the COVID-19 pandemic. Success starts at the top, and while ownership deserves enormous credit for the on- and off-the-field turnaround, much credit goes to Peter Vermes and the great players who became stars in Kansas City—such as Graham Zusi, Benny Feilhaber, Roger Espinoza, Matt Besler, Ike Opara, Johnny Russell and goalkeepers Jimmy Nielsen and Tim Melia, to name just a few.

As a personal aside, in reading this book, my thoughts often turned to the late Neal Patterson. Neal was a great partner with Cliff and the rest of the Sporting ownership group, and we all owe a debt of gratitude for his belief in MLS and his commit ment to the Kansas City community. We all miss him. Like Lamar Hunt in the early days of the club, Sporting Kansas City does not become the admired organization and community partner it is without Neal. I'm glad this book will forever be a reminder of Neal's legacy with Sporting and in MLS.

From the team's birth to its revival and numerous triumphs, this book covers it all. It is for the fans, but it is also about the fans. Because the supporters of Sporting Kansas City are as much a part of the club's amazing story as anyone.

"I Believe That We Will Win!"

This book shows why the soccer fans of Kansas City are justified in their belief that anything is possible. I hope you take pride in that, and cherish every word, every image, every memory.

1996-2006

THE BE

GINNING

More than a decade after the demise of the North American Soccer League, professional soccer returned to the United States. Coming in the wake of the wildly successful 1994 World Cup—the first on American soil—Major League Soccer launched in 1996, determined to bring the world's game to a new generation of fans. Amid all the optimism and excitement there remained the nagging question: Could soccer finally establish itself as a major sport in the States? And, closer to home, was Kansas City ready for its own MLS team?

GROWING PAINS

BY ANY NAME, A ROUGH START

The famed Palladium concert hall and nightclub in New York City had seen its share of flashy shows, but it had never seen anything quite like this. As ABC Sports host Roger Twibell strolled to the lectern at center stage, he was surrounded on all sides by the best light and laser displays the mid-1990s had to offer. To his left and right were large 5-by-5 banks of televisions, flashing logos in a checkered pattern, and behind him was a giant, 25-foot-tall screen filled edge-to-edge with the blue and green logo of Major League Soccer, America's new first-division outdoor professional soccer league. A big logo for a big announcement. Today, Oct. 17, 1995, was the day the world would finally hear the names and see the logos of the nascent league's 10 teams, who would begin play the following spring.

"A special applause for my hometown of Kansas City," he said as he listed off the cities and invited their new stars to the stage to join him alongside U.S. Soccer's Alan Rothenberg. There were Alexi Lalas, Tony Meola and John Harkes, members of the 1994 U.S. World Cup team, with videos showcasing their highlights. Flashy Mexican goalkeeper/striker Jorge Campos and Bolivian midfield maestro Marco Etcheverry had videos as well. Last to the stage was Mike Sorber, another member of the 1994 U.S. team. Sorber didn't have an accompanying video, or even a graphic. He had been allocated to Kansas City.

"Now, with the help of some magical, mystical inspiration, we bring you Kansas City: The home of the Kansas City Wiz!"

The franchise was off to an ignominious start.

The names, logos and uniforms of the original 10 Major League Soccer teams made their debut on Oct. 17, 1995 at the Palladium night club in New York City at "MLS Unveiled."

The KC Spurs called Kansas City home for two years in 1969 and '70, and the Comets briefly made indoor soccer an entertainment phenomenon in in the '80s and early '90s.

The announcement set off a sprint to the league's inaugural game just 10 months later. However, the birth of Major League Soccer and its 10 original teams can be traced back to the most important day in American soccer history: July 4, 1988. The day when FIFA Executive Vice President Harry Cavan announced: "The host country for the 1994 World Cup will be the United States of America."

At a period when the U.S. was without a first division outdoor professional league after the North American Soccer League folded following its 1984 season, the United States' 381-page bid book included a pledge to put in place a new professional league.

While Arrowhead Stadium, one of 18 proposed venues in the bid, would ultimately miss out on hosting matches, the record-setting success of the 1994 World Cup would indeed spark renewed interest in American soccer and fulfill its promise of launching a professional domestic league. It also proved decisive in securing Lamar Hunt's investment in the league, according to his son Clark.

"It really wasn't until after the World Cup, which was so successful, that I think caused another lightbulb to go off in my dad's head to say, 'Hey, I think it might be time to give it another go.'"

Hunt, as owner of the Kansas City Chiefs, had been an important figure in the city for decades, and had long been committed to promoting soccer in America. He owned the NASL's Dallas Tornado from 1967-1981 and served as chairman of the NASL. MLS officials had been in discussions with Lamar Hunt for more than two years and when they introduced the league's first four investors on Nov. 16, 1994, the Hunt family was a natural inclusion.

However, Lamar Hunt was the only one not aligned with a team.

"We've given him a list of cities we'd be happy with and if he picks any of those, that will be fine with us," MLS Chairman Alan Rothenberg said.

League officials had begun identifying prospective markets for MLS clubs dating back to Dec. 17, 1993, when the MLS logo was unveiled in conjunction with the 1994 World Cup draw in Las Vegas.

"It was a very exciting time," said MLS President Mark Abbott, who was a senior vice president for business development at the time. "There was a FIFA executive committee meeting where Alan presented the basic business plan for what became MLS. And immediately after that, we went into a press conference where Alan announced that FIFA had reviewed and approved the plan that we had put in place for what ultimately would become the league."

Forty-three cities were on the league's initial franchise list and Kansas City was among 29 hopeful markets that sent representatives to the MLS Bidders Conference in January 1994. By March 1994, Arrowhead Stadium was confirmed as the centerpiece of Kansas City's application to MLS, boosted by the decision a month earlier to install natural grass for the first time since the venue opened in 1972.

Kansas City's broader professional soccer history was similarly limited. The Spurs won a NASL title in 1969, but folded after the 1970 season—a fate not unfamiliar to Kansas City, which lost major league teams in the 1960s (MLB's KC Athletics), 1970s (NHL's KC Scouts) and 1980s (NBA's KC Kings). Professional soccer in Kansas City went dark until the Comets lit up Kemper Arena in 1981. A decade later, the MSL All-Star Game was held in Kansas City in 1991 as indoor soccer rode a wave of highs and lows throughout the 1980s and 1990s.

Now came an opportunity to be part of Major League Soccer in the afterglow of the World Cup.

In April 1995, Hunt revealed—almost as an afterthought at a press conference for legendary NFL and Chiefs quarterback Joe Montana's retirement—that he was investing in MLS teams in both Kansas City and Columbus.

"Initially we had planned to have one team," Hunt later explained. "But partially to help Major League Soccer, we ended up with two teams. We studied 14 different markets. From the beginning, Kansas City was where we wanted to be."

Kansas City had a venue. It had an investor. And two months later, KC officially had its team. In short order, the club's infrastructure was built from scratch with general manager Tim Latta and head coach Ron Newman appointed as the architects.

It also had a name. The "Wiz" moniker, ridiculed by pundits, emerged from a name-the-team contest that began in the *Kansas City Star* on June 8, 1995. More than 3,200 entries were submitted with six suggesting Wizards as the team name, including Lee's Summit, Missouri, 9-year-old Sarah Starr who was chosen as the promotion's grand prize winner. (Four other names were also considered as finalists: Quest, Rivercats, Roughriders and Twisters.)

The name was not well received. A local graphic artist redesigned the team's logo to feature a toilet, long before an area plumber flew a banner over Arrowhead for the team's inaugural game, which produced this incomparable quote from Latta to clear the air on any misconceptions.

"We are definitely not a urinal. Arrowhead will not be the Yellow Brick Road. Dorothy and the Tin Man will not be our mascots." The team's inaugural marketing slogan, pitched by a local ad agency, didn't help the cause. "You gotta go," lasted only days before getting the proverbial flush.

Why Wiz and not Wizards? And why did the team make the change to the Wizards following the 1996 season?

"Our original desire was to use the name Wizards … but the Delaware Wizards [of the USISL] held the trademark rights to the name," Latta said. "After discussions with our equipment supplier, the decision was made to go with the shortened version Wiz, which followed the league's progressive marketing approach." Later, the East Coast electronics firm Nobody Beats the Wiz Inc. charged that the team was infringing on their copyright, while the team in Delaware eventually relinquished their claim to Wizards. So after their first season, the Wiz became the Wizards.

When Sorber took the stage at the MLS brand unveiling—introduced as Kansas City's first of five allocated players—he was wearing the club's then-mocked, now iconic rainbow kit, featuring the team's official Carolina blue and black primary colors. While Sorber played professionally in Mexico, Kansas City's four additional allocated players would all come from European leagues: Frank Klopas, Vitalis "Digital" Takawira, Predrag "Preki" Radosavljevic and Mo Johnston.

They would help lead the club to a 17-15 record in 1996, including nine come-from-behind victories and five wins coming via shootout. Shootouts were one of two major adaptations MLS implemented—after considering many others, including increasing the size of the goals—and were used to decide any game ending in a draw. With the ball 35 yards from goal, each shooter would have five seconds to score in a best-of-five format. Teams were awarded three points for a win in regulation and one point for a win via shootout.

In the other major departure from the global game, each half in MLS matches started with the clock at 45:00 and counted down to zero. The referee could signal the timekeeper to stop the clock, and there was no stoppage time added to the end of halves.

Kansas City's 1996 season kicked off on April 13 with a 3-0 win over the Colorado Rapids in front of 21,141 fans for the inaugural game at Arrowhead, highlighted by two goals from Takawira and one from Klopas.

Soccer team's 'You Gotta Go' slogan is down the drain

HEARNE
Christopher Jr.

That giant sucking sound?

Could be the sound of the KC Wiz extinguishing the team's new ad slogan.

It had a shelf life of three days, tops.

"A season of Soccer Sorcery awaits Kansas City," Wiz GM **Tim Latta** wrote in a Feb. 16 letter to season ticket holders. "And as the ads will say, 'You Gotta Go!' "

Oops! Lavatory humor alert.

Those much-cackled-about, go-to-the-bathroom jokes that have been so wildly popular with the sports talk set since the team announced its name last fall are back. At least they were.

On Monday the Wiz decided to give the new tag a fast flush.

"We can't control other people doing it, but we're not going to instigate it," says Wiz PR guy **Jim Moorhouse**, referring to the somewhat obvious potty humor. "**Barkley & Evergreen** pitched it to us last week and we were intrigued by it. They love it, and they were thinking, 'That's going to get us publicity.' But we've decided to not go down that road."

"I'll be honest; I'm surprised they went with it (initially)," says B&E executive VP **Scott Aylward**. "That's a rather traditional line in sports. But (with the Wiz) it has a little more flavor."

Maybe next time.

Frank Klopas in 1996; The KC Star's report on the demise of the original Wiz marketing slogan.

"The thing I will always remember is that I was the first one to score a goal in the history of the club," said Takawira, who celebrated with his "Digital Crawl" along the touchline—a celebration that would soon become all the rage for 12-year-olds across Kansas City, and prompt the team to take out billboards promoting it. "That will always be in my heart, and I will always cherish that moment."

The Wiz won three of the team's first four games, including a 6-4 barnburner over Columbus on May 2 that remains the second-highest scoring match in MLS history. Preki would score in five straight games in June, and the club climbed into first place in the Western Conference in late August. However, three losses in the final four games—and a league worst 63 goals conceded—dropped the Wiz to third in the table.

KC had logged 250 shots on goal in their maiden season, a regular season record that still stands 25 years later, and that offensive firepower carried into the postseason as the Wiz produced a dramatic 3-2 comeback win over the Dallas Burn on an 89th-minute goal from Preki. The late game-winner, made possible by Sean Bowers' incredible goal line clearance 20 minutes earlier, came on the team's 15th shot on goal of the match, a postseason record that stood until 2019.

The following week, Kansas City clinched the best-of-three series in a penalty shootout in the decisive third game. Advancing to the Conference Finals, the match-up with the first-place LA Galaxy was played under controversial circumstances. The start of the series was moved back to accommodate Galaxy players competing in World Cup qualifying and the home-away format was altered due to the Rose Bowl's availability.

The Wiz fell 2-1 in the opener on the road before succumbing in a penalty shootout in the home leg after Takawira's go-ahead goal with 45 seconds remaining was ruled offside. Preki was selected to the MLS Best XI and would become an American citizen in the offseason, finally making him eligible for a U.S. Men's National Team debut.

The Wizards enjoyed a strong sophomore season in 1997, going 21-11 (with a league-best seven shootout wins) and finished atop the Western Conference. The additions of U.S. international Steve Pittman and Scottish international Richard Gough bolstered the backline, while Mike Ammann took over in net after the departure of Garth Lagerwey.

The team's attack was again led by the midfield duo of Preki and Chung, who combined for 26 goals and 22 assists in 1996 but still couldn't be stopped in 1997 as together they tallied 22 goals and 25 assists.

Preki was the league's scoring champion and Most Valuable Player with 12 goals and 17 assists while again earning MLS Best XI recognition along with Chung and Gough.

Similar to 1996, the Wizards won three of their first four and lost three of their last four—this time with a seven-game winning streak sandwiched in the summer, including an eventful skirmish on July 4 against the Columbus Crew that capped off a run of five straight victories on the road.

Five days before coaching the Western Conference in the MLS All-Star Game, Newman was ejected from the sidelines of Ohio Stadium and subsequently produced one of the more memorable disciplinary decisions: MLS fined Kansas City coach Ron Newman $1,500 for his physical confrontation with Crew midfielder Marcelo Carrera, his attempts to provoke a fight with several Columbus players and his foul language.

As he was escorted off the field by two officers, Newman adjusted his tie, smiled for the broadcast camera and held up his fingers to indicate the score: Kansas City 2, Columbus 1.

Antics aside, KC would fall in the postseason to the eventual MLS Cup runners-up for a second straight year.

In 1997 it came in the Western Conference Semifinals versus Colorado. The Rapids had finished fourth in the West and had lost all four games in the regular season series but swept KC aside with a 3-0 win at Arrowhead and a 3-2 win in the return leg.

Off the field, the 1997 campaign saw Kansas City slip to last in the league in attendance—a spot the club would remain in for three straight seasons—with just over 9,000 fans at Arrowhead on game days, despite the lowest average ticket price in the league.

Struggles at the box office weren't unique to the Wizards. After exceeding expectations with an average attendance of 17,406 fans in 1996, the league's attendance declined to 14,619 in 1997. The Americanization of the sport wasn't providing the desired effect of pulling more casual sports fans to games, and in fact may have turned off traditional soccer fans and players alike. The league was struggling to build an identity and fan experience.

"I believed in the potential of the product," Lamar Hunt wrote in Major League Soccer's book *A Celebration of 10 Seasons*. "I'm not sure we adequately gauged the difficulty of playing in overly large American football stadiums."

Entire sections of seats were tarped off for MLS matches at Arrowhead to reduce its capacity from 79,101 to 20,571 and, despite the best efforts of the Samba Fan Club and Mystics supporters groups to improve the atmosphere, the situation wasn't ideal.

Peter Wilt, GM of the Chicago Fire, once recalled hearing Wizards GM Tim Latta on a walkie-talkie instructing security to throw fans out of the stadium. They'd been tossing confetti and as Latta said, "It's so expensive to clean up after games."

A new general manager, Doug Newman, was hired in the buildup to the 1998 season, but he

Opposite: Digital Takawira dribbling against Brad Wilson of the Los Angeles Galaxy, Aug. 21, 1996. The Wizards won 5-4 in a shootout after a 1-1 draw. Below: Head Coach Ron Newman was the winningest coach in indoor soccer history, and the first coach named in MLS.

would have a new challenge to face in his two-year stint with the club: A slumping team that lost more often than it won.

After a first-place finish in 1997, the Wizards—who added St. Louis native Chris Klein and Kansas City native Scott Vermillion, as well as former Everton striker Paul Rideout—finished last in 1998 with a 12-20 record.

Preki was one of two Wizards players selected to participate in the 1998 World Cup in France, making two appearances for the United States while Okafor started once for the Super Eagles of Nigeria.

But arguably the most notable development of 1998 came in the summer when the Wizards finally found a permanent training ground in Swope Park. "We were like nomads going from one place to another looking for good training facilities," remembered Bowers, Kansas City's Defender of the Year in 1996 and 1997. "Sometimes the grass was up to your ankles." The team had gone through 11 practice sites midway through its second season, including UMKC, Johnson County Community College, Blue Valley North High School, The Barstow School and Raytown South High School.

"Public parks, community colleges, we'd get places where we'd get a lease for a month and then move on again. We'd train indoors for a month at a time. You name it, we tried it," said Lagerwey.

Now the Wizards had their own practice facility on a site previously used as the offices and training home for the Kansas City Chiefs from 1963 to 1972 (and just down the road from the Kansas City Zoo, where the Wizards infamous 1999 team photo was taken inside the elephant exhibit).

Behind the scenes, the Wizards operation as a business was at a critical juncture. Lamar Hunt had been diagnosed with prostate cancer in September 1998 and was undergoing treatment. In an effort to both liven things up and save on budget, the Wizards merged the club's marketing and promotions department with those of the Chiefs prior to the 1999 season. The team was simultaneously under scrutiny from league officials, including MLS Commissioner Doug Logan.

"I think all the right things are in place," Logan told The *Kansas City Star*. "If that doesn't translate into at least some increased numbers through the turnstiles, then we've certainly got to feel we've done everything we could and start scratching our heads and wondering if it might not work better someplace else."

The team needed to make a splash to start the 1999 season and did so on Jan. 28 with "the biggest, and most surprising, swap of players in Major League Soccer history" to that point. Alexi Lalas and Tony Meola, two of the most recognizable individuals in American soccer, were headed to Kansas City. All-Stars in each of the league's first three seasons and U.S. Men's National Team standouts, the duo brought an instant buzz.

The Star wrote of Lalas, "He's here to save professional soccer. There's really no other way to put it. Will he draw fans in Kansas City? Well, he's already more recognizable than any player on the Royals and just about anyone on the Chiefs. There's a buzz around the Wizards that has not been there since they came into town three years ago, a genuine excitement because Lalas is a genuine star. At a time when Kansas City sports teams are notably short on star power, the most famous local athlete is a soccer player."

Alas, things didn't go according to plan. Meola, who required 35 stitches in his mouth on March 13 while playing for the U.S., tore his ACL in practice with the Wizards, three days before the March 20 season opener.

The team went through eight goalkeepers on the roster by the second game of the season. Ron Newman—one of only two coaches still with their original club at the start of 1999—stepped down after the fourth game, replaced by interim manager Ken Fogarty.

The Wizards lost their first seven games and its last seven games, ending the year 8-24. To cap it off, Lalas—then 29 years old—announced he was retiring in the locker room immediately after the season finale.

No one could have predicted, at the end of a dismal 1999, the fairytale turnaround in store as the team entered the new millennium. ♦

Opposite: Chopper the Dragon and a Wizards Girl cheerleader before a match; fans wave promotional gate giveaway blue pool noodles. Below: Before their rise to fame during the 2010 World Cup in South Africa, vuvuzela noisemakers were all the rage with kids at early MLS matches.

KANSAS CITY
WIZ
adidas
11

MY STORY: PREKI

"Even though I work for the Seattle Sounders now, I still have a soft spot in my heart for Sporting KC. That's the club that I spent nine seasons playing for, and I have some incredible memories from my time in Kansas City. That's my team.

My wife and I loved Kansas City—it was a great place to raise kids, and we thoroughly enjoyed our time there. The only thing I didn't like about playing at Arrowhead Stadium is that the field itself was very small. In the big football stadiums in Europe, the dimensions would be much larger—120 yards by 75 yards—and even though Arrowhead had a long field, it was really narrow.

I have great memories of the Wizards fans. They were very respectful, and the fans appreciated what I did on the pitch, and I appreciated them, so it was a really good relationship. You could say maybe I played there at the wrong time because of how things are now with Sporting KC in terms of the packed stadium and everything like that but even in my time, it was great. Unfortunately, we didn't have a following like Sporting KC has today—they are selling out every game. But at Arrowhead, a lot of games we would get 10,000—12,000 people, and the stadium was so big it looked like almost no one was there.

I don't know if I felt like a "star" when I played for the Wizards, but I didn't really think about things like that. I'm the kind of person who doesn't love getting a ton of attention. I'm a pretty quiet person. I liked to be recognized on game day when I was playing, but in my free time, I liked just being a normal guy, and I was able to do that in Kansas City.

Speaking of being a normal guy, my gym and my basketball games were among my favorite things in Kansas City! There was a great group of guys, and I miss those basketball games dearly. Basketball was actually my first love, but I recognized as a teenager that I wasn't going to grow much taller, so I decided to focus on soccer.

I played basketball mainly in the off season because I didn't want to risk getting injured during the season. We didn't have any restrictions on what we did in our free time—no one from the Wizards ever told me I should stop playing basketball—and I actually played basketball with a lot of football players, including Will Shields from the Chiefs. I figured if they could play, why couldn't I play? I wouldn't say I was a dominating basketball player, but I could definitely hold my own.

When I was traded to Miami after the 2000 season, I never thought I would come back and play for the Wizards again. It wasn't my decision to leave, and when somebody trades you, usually that means that the franchise is done with you. But that didn't end up being the case. When Miami folded, I got drafted by Kansas City, and that was a great thing for me and my family. My family had never moved from Kansas City during my season with Miami, so that worked out really well for us.

At first, I had hard feelings about the organization trading me, but I'm not the kind of person who holds grudges. When I came back, the first day I talked to coach Bob Gansler and I told him "Bob, I don't want to talk about it, it's in the past. It's behind us, so let's move forward and see what we can do to win again." That was my attitude, and we never spoke of the trade again.

People ask me how I was able to play at such a high level as I got older, and a lot of that boils down to what you want. I wanted to play! I loved competing, and I felt I had more left in the tank. I did everything possible to extend my career—I started doing yoga, and I also focused a lot on my diet. I also have to give a lot of credit to my wife and my family. My wife was very supportive, and we had a very stable family, and if your family is in a good place, then your mind is in a good place, and in that situation, I feel that anything can be achieved.

2000 MLS Cup
2000 Supporters' Shield
2004 US Open Cup

Preki is the only two-time MLS MVP Award and MLS Scoring Champion Award winner. He also represented the United States at the 1998 FIFA World Cup, was named to the MLS All-Time Best XI team and was inducted into the National Soccer Hall of Fame in 2010.

ARROWHEAD STADIUM

1996 - 2007

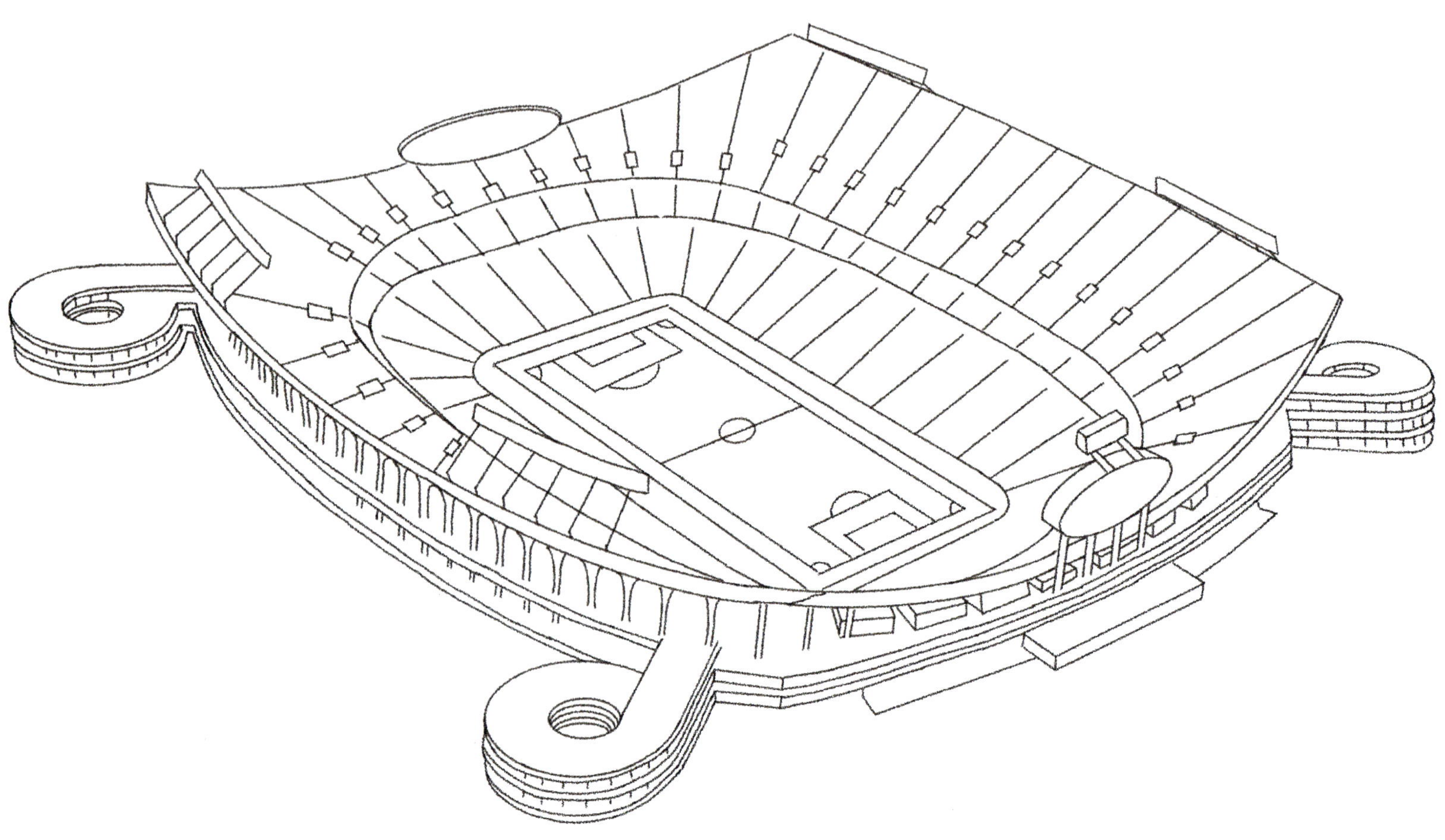

79,451

STADIUM CAPACITY

11,048

AVERAGE ATTENDANCE

102-57-25

RECORD [W-L-T]

"My first thought walking onto the field at Arrowhead Stadium was "Wow, look at the size of this place." It was a beautiful stadium, but it looked pretty empty. Don't get me wrong ... it's always great playing in a big stadium, but preferably you want your stadium packed. You want everything compact, you want the fans on top of you and you want the atmosphere. But going back to 1996, that just isn't the way it was in MLS—the teams couldn't build their own stadiums that quickly."

—MO JOHNSTON

adidas

MY STORY: MO JOHNSTON

"I knew absolutely nothing about Kansas City before I got here. Not a thing. But I got a call in April of 1996 to see if I wanted to come to Kansas City on trial, and I said absolutely! I jumped on a plane that night, then I trained with the guys the next morning and then two days later I played in a game against Columbus at Arrowhead [the fourth game of the inaugural 1996 MLS season].

We won that game 6-4 and I scored a couple of goals. I had always wanted to try and play in the U.S. I didn't really know much about my teammates going into that game, but football is football at the end of the day. It was 11 v 11 and there were fans in the stadium, and after that first game, I felt like I had landed with a good team.

It was different back then in the first few years of MLS, and I thought the shootouts were strange. I remember the first time in training that we practiced the shootout, and I thought the idea was just to go and beat the goalkeeper, but later I realized that we only had five seconds to score. That part was strange to me, and I was disqualified the first time I ever was part of a shootout for starting too soon.

I absolutely loved Kansas City, and I still have friends there. That's where my three kids were born, and I was with Kansas City longer than I was with any other club during my career—I think that kind of tells you something. Even today, I still love to watch my Chiefs! I used to try and get to most Chiefs games even if we played away on a Saturday—I just loved going to those games. Tony Gonzalez lived four doors down from me in Overland Park. The Chiefs also had Lawrence Tynes back then, who was a Scottish kicker. I made him walk out of the tunnel with us one game, which was fun.

My favorite game I ever played in Kansas City was the game where I got my eye busted open to set up the winning goal against LA—the 2000 Western Conference Championship. I knew I had to do what I did on that play, and I knew there were going to be consequences because I would be taking a cleat straight to the face. You could see that the Galaxy player was getting ready to put his cleat up, and the only option I had was to put my head in front of his foot and get the ball to Miklos Molnar. That decision led to an all-time goal—the goal that got us through to MLS Cup, and we ended up winning the championship—so it was totally worth the cuts on my face and all the blood. Most of the injuries in my soccer career happened in Kansas City, which is funny, and I needed about 18 stitches on my face after that game.

I had the chance to tour the Sporting KC facilities with Peter Vermes a few years ago, and it's just night and day compared to the facilities we had the first few years in MLS. When I played here, all the players had to change in a porta-cabin when we practiced in Swope Park. The first time I saw that I was like, "Holy shit, what's this?" But we just adapted and we went with it. There were 28 other players sitting in a porta-cabin doing the exact same thing, so why would I complain. Things like that didn't really bother me, because I knew that eventually we were going to get to go on the field and play football. A lot of other MLS teams back then had a similar setup, and some were even worse!

I love coming back to Kansas City, and I was there the last time they won a championship—it was great seeing everybody so happy. And I'm glad I was able to get Johnny Russell to Kansas City. I called Peter and said, "You need to sign this player. He's very good, and he's great in the locker room. The fans will love him, you will love him and the guys in the dressing room will love him." I'm proud of how well Johnny has done with the club. Even if you take soccer out of it, Johnny is a fantastic guy. He's the kind of guy that can be a team captain, and he's just a guy you can really rely on.

2000 MLS Cup
2000 Supporters' Shield

Mo Johnston joined Celtic F.C. in 1984 and scored 72 goals in 128 matches, won the Scottish Cup in 1985 and the Scottish Championship in 1986. Johnston signed with Rangers in 1989 and won two Scottish league titles with the team, scoring 46 goals in 100 games. Mo finished his career with the Wizards, scoring 31 goals for the club in 149 games and helping lead them to the 2000 MLS Cup championship. Johnston also scored 14 goals in 38 appearances for Scotland, including one at the 1990 FIFA World Cup.

SNAPSHOT
THE WIZ
1995-1996

1) Wiz foam finger, circa 1996

2) Printer's proofs of original inaugural season ticket design, rejected by Lamar Hunt for use of Wizard imagery

3) Archive photo of the 1996 Wiz front-office staff

4) Screen-printed gate giveaway Wiz flag

5) Wiz marketing stickers, circa 1996 featuring rarely used secondary logo

6) Press release announcing the name change from Wiz to Wizards due to threat of lawsuit, Nov. 18, 1996

1

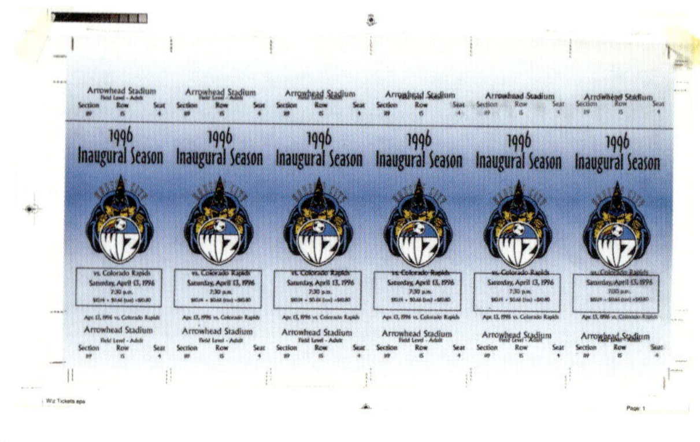

2

3

4

5

Media Release

For Immediate Release
November 18, 1996

WIZARDS ™

Contact: Jim Moorhouse
816/472-4625 x108
or 913/671-7492

KANSAS CITY IS NOW HOME OF THE WIZARDS

Major League Soccer's "Wiz" Officially Extend Name to "Wizards"

The Kansas City Wizards is the new name of Major League Soccer's Kansas City franchise. Known by the short name Wiz during the club's inaugural 1996 season, the club officially extended their name to Wizards in an announcement today.

"The new name was a result of several factors coinciding," said General Manager Tim Latta. "Our original desire was to use the name Wizards as a result of the '1995 Name the Team' contest, but the Delaware Wizards soccer team of the United Systems of Independent Soccer Leagues (Division 3 Outdoor) held the trademark rights to the name. After discussions with our equipment supplier, the decision was made to go with the shortened version Wiz, which followed the League's progressive marketing approach.

"After we announced the team name, the Eastern-based electronics firm 'Nobody Beats The Wiz Inc.' expressed concern that we may be infringing upon their trademark rights to the name Wiz. With the success of MLS in its inaugural season, the Delaware Wizards have since indicated their desire to help support the League and the sport, and have released their claim to provide the MLS full and permanent approval to use the name Wizards."

Latta, a successful pro soccer manager for the last five years, concluded by saying: "In looking at our options, we felt it was important to keep the spirit of the original name intact, so with input from the local community and others involved, the decision has now been made to adapt the Kansas City name to Wizards."

As part of the name change, the club has also modified their popular, visual logo. The team crest now features the Wizards moniker in a geometric shape, with their familiar soccer ball and rainbow trail still centered at the top. The team's primary colors remain Carolina blue and black.

During their inaugural season, the Kansas City MLS team was a hit both on the field and at the turnstiles. The club averaged 12,901 fans per game and advanced to the MLS Final Four, losing to the Los Angeles Galaxy in the Western Conference Finals. Behind the club's top players, Preki and Digital Takawira, the Wiz were the highest scoring team at home, averaging 2.5 goals per game every time they took the field at Arrowhead Stadium.

For head coach Ron Newman, who has proven to be a wizard at every level of pro coaching in America, he now has a new challenge by the same name.

"The new name is a perfect fit for us," said Newman. "Sir Stanley Matthews of England was known as the 'Wizard of Dribble' and that certainly fits Preki today. You can expect great 'Feets of Magic' from the Wizards in 1997 at Arrowhead."

Kansas City Wizards 1997 season tickets are on sale now. Call 816/472-GOAL for more information.

— K.C. Wizards —

KANSAS CITY WIZARDS

706 Broadway Suite 100
Kansas City, Mo 64105-2300
816/472-GOAL • 816/472-0299 FAX

6

adidas
WIZARDS
KANSAS CITY
5

MY STORY: KERRY ZAVAGNIN

I arrived in Kansas City in 2000, at the crossroads of my career. After spending time on the bench with the New York/New Jersey MetroStars, I decided to go play in the second division for the Lehigh Valley Steam and better establish my career as a professional. At the end of my first season with Lehigh in late 1999, I started making calls around MLS to try and join a team for preseason camp. All I wanted was an opportunity. Fortunately, Bob Gansler gave me that opportunity.

Shortly after I got to Florida for preseason training, I had a meeting with coach Gansler at his "office by the pool." I told him all of my objectives—that I wanted to be a starter in MLS, play on a successful team and win championships. I told him that if I was good enough, I wanted that opportunity to be on the field. It's pretty simple to say that as a player, but it's another thing for the coach to believe in you and for the player to live up to that.

Before I came to Kansas City, I really knew very little about the city or the team. Shortly after I got here, I remember the Plaza being my world. I lived there, and I really did not venture far from the Plaza other than for training. The Plaza was the epicenter of the city at that time, and I loved it.

I had come from the East Coast, a place where the sports fans are much different. I was pleasantly surprised that our fans were so appreciative of you as a player—win, lose or draw. That was different. At the same time, there weren't a ton of Wizards fans. You had to be there to understand how vacant Arrowhead Stadium was for many games. Peter Vermes and I have a great picture of us walking off the field after warm-ups, and we're pretty sure it was a playoff game, and you maybe see three people in the background and a ton of empty orange seats. This was right before kickoff. The people who did come to the games and supported us were amazing.

As I mentioned, the Plaza was the center of my life during my time with the Wizards, and that included my gameday routine. When I look back on it, it was completely contrary to what sports science today would suggest that you do. The night before the game I would eat a steak at Capital Grille. That was my pregame routine, and I was very specific with that. Postgame was a different story. I don't say this in an arrogant way, but we had some teams back then where we assumed that we were going to win the game that day, and we did win a lot of our home games. After our wins, we would always go to Figlio's for a postgame meal and then we would go out on the Plaza. Those were great times.

While it wasn't the venue I wish I would have concluded my career in, CommunityAmerica Ballpark was a stepping stone to bigger and better things for our organization. I'll never forget the tifo the fans created honoring me before my last home game for the club. It was an authentic, genuine and heartfelt show of appreciation.

It wasn't out of convenience that I stayed in Kansas City after I retired. It was because I understood that there was a vision and a project that was in the process of being fulfilled, and I wanted to be a part of that and see the fruits of the labor. This has been one of the most rewarding experiences that I have ever had. Just think about it: The Wizards almost relocated. In a league that wasn't on sound footing, our organization was at the very bottom in terms of stability. The turnaround our organization made is the ultimate success story of Major League Soccer. Sporting Kansas City has done something that no other club has accomplished, and the people of Kansas City understand that, which is really cool.

AS PLAYER

2000 MLS Cup
2000 Supporters' Shield
2004 U.S. Open Cup

AS COACH

2012 U.S. Open Cup
2013 MLS Cup
2015 U.S. Open Cup
2017 U.S. Open Cup

Kerry Zavagnin played in 237 games (228 starts) and logged 20,515 minutes for the Wizards, setting team records in both categories. Zavagnin was named the Team Defender of the Year in 2001, a member of the MLS Best XI team in 2004 and also appeared 21 times for the United States Men's National Team.

The Wizards starting lineup for the 2000 MLS Cup was Head Coach Bob Gansler's preferred lineup throughout the season. Front row (L to R): Preki, Chris Henderson, Brandon Prideaux, Peter Vermes, Nick Garica; Back row: Tony Meola, Kerry Zavagnin, Chris Klein, Miklos Molnar, Mo Johnston and Matt McKeon

WIZARDS AT WORK

THE MAGICAL 2000 SEASON

Bob Gansler faced a steep, uphill climb.

Appointed by general manager Doug Newman and owner Lamar Hunt as the Wizards' second head coach in April of 1999, Gansler was tasked with resurrecting a club that had finished last in the Western Conference the previous year and dropped each of its first seven matches at that point in the 1999 campaign.

Just four seasons into its existence, the club had been dubiously labeled a small-market cellar dweller.

As precarious as the situation was, Gansler relished the opportunity. The Hungary-born defender played for the United States in the 1960s, served as a U.S. Soccer coaching director in the 1970s and led the U.S. U-19s and U-20s in the 1980s. Following a stint at the University of Wisconsin-Milwaukee from 1984-1988, Gansler was selected as head coach of the U.S. Men's National Team in 1989 and promptly led the Americans to the 1990 FIFA World Cup in Italy, marking the country's first appearance at the tournament in 40 years. In 1997, Gansler led the second-division Milwaukee Rampage to an A-League championship.

Perhaps just as importantly, Gansler had a chip on his shoulder.

Legendary American soccer coach Bob Gansler completely rebuilt the Wizards roster around veteran players with whom he had history – and faith.

"When MLS began in 1996, I was disappointed not to be one of the original head coaches in the league," Gansler said. "Sometimes life isn't fair and sometimes soccer isn't fair. But I arrived in Kansas City determined to prove myself. Over time we welcomed a lot of players who felt the same way."

The Wizards endured a forgettable 1999 season, finishing with eight wins and a club-record 24 losses. From there Gansler orchestrated one of the greatest and most unlikely turnarounds in MLS history.

In the fateful months that followed, Gansler and assistant coach Brian Bliss rebuilt the team around a squad of reliable holdovers, then ventured out to find some key additions.

"The players who formed the core of our team in 2000 were left frustrated by the past," Gansler said. "We had a blue-collar mentality, and we were determined to show others what we were capable of. That was a powerful combination."

The first step was ensuring that key pieces from the 1999 team returned to the club. That group included highlight-reel playmaker and 1997 MLS MVP Preki, the vibrant Scottish forward Mo Johnston, and hard-working wide midfielders Chris Henderson and Chris Klein.

Keeping U.S. international goalkeeper Tony Meola was another major priority. Meola had been traded from his hometown New York/New Jersey MetroStars to the Wizards in 1999—a move he was less than happy about. A few weeks before the season began, Meola was scrimmaging as a field player at practice and suffered an ACL injury that sidelined him for most of the year. When Gansler arrived as the new coach, he and Meola had a candid conversation. Meola told him he wanted to be traded back East following the 1999 season, and the manager seemed receptive.

But after seeing Meola return to action for the last nine games of the '99 season, Gansler called and made his case to Meola: "Tony, I know I said we would trade you back to New York, but hear me out. We're bringing in some great players that you know well, and I need you to come back for one more year. We'll restructure your contract and give you a little more money. Stay in Kansas City, give me one solid year and then I'll trade you back to New York. You have my word."

With that, the deal was struck. "Bob was someone I really respected," Meola said. "So I agreed to come back. It proved to be one of the best decisions I've ever made."

As Kansas City entered the new millennium, Gansler's attention turned toward acquiring experienced players who could make an instant impact. Two marquee newcomers arrived from the Colorado Rapids: Peter Vermes, a World Cup veteran center back whose fierce competitiveness matched his pedigree, and Matt McKeon, a no-nonsense midfielder who'd previously played in Kansas City from 1996-1998. Gansler had coached Vermes and Meola at the 1990 World Cup and knew McKeon from his time as a U.S. U-16 youth national teamer.

To bolster the attack, Gansler signed prolific Danish striker Miklos Molnar, a journeyman who had previous spells in Denmark, Belgium, Switzerland, France, Germany and Spain. Henderson, who played with Molnar at German club FSV Frankfurt from 1994-1995, helped convince the forward to make the move stateside.

In the 2000 MLS SuperDraft, the Wizards took two-time NCAA national champion defender Nick Garcia from Indiana and industrious midfielder Kerry Zavagnin, a member of the MetroStars from 1997-1998, who had spent 1999 with the second-division Lehigh Valley Steam.

"When we all got together during preseason, we began calling ourselves the castaways," Meola said.

A consistent lineup was key to success throughout the season. The midfield quintet of Kerry Zavagnin, Preki, Chris Henderson, Matt McKeon and Chris Klein (not pictured) started 25 of 32 regular season matches together, as well as every postseason match.

"We would joke about that all the time—the fact that we weren't wanted at our previous clubs. But very quickly you could start to see that we were building something really special. With the leaders we had on the team, the culture of the club changed so quickly."

The outsized personalities of Vermes, Meola, Johnston and Preki made for a lively team dynamic.

"We weren't afraid to say things that needed to be said, and sometimes they weren't nice things," Vermes said. "The entire group held each other accountable every single day. If you weren't there with an unrelenting desire to compete and win, you weren't going to fit in."

WORST TO FIRST

A demanding preseason camp saw the Wizards train in Florida before heading south to Bolivia to compete at elevations well over a mile high. Upon returning to Kansas City, Gansler had settled on a 4-4-2 formation with Vermes, Garcia, much-improved second-year player Brandon Prideaux and veteran Uche Okafor along the backline. When Okafor came down with the shingles virus, Gansler was forced to readjust and shifted to a 3-5-2 formation the week before the season opener. It wound up being the formation they would play throughout the season.

"In many ways, it was a setup that maximized our potential on the field," Zavagnin said. "Matt McKeon and I protected the back three as holding midfielders, Henderson and Klein covered a ton of ground as the wide midfielders, Preki and Mo were the attacking playmakers and Miklos was the clinical goal scorer."

On March 25, with 7,540 fans in attendance at Arrowhead Stadium, the Wizards delivered a warning sign to the rest of MLS with a wild 4-3 victory over the star-studded Chicago Fire. Molnar scored early in his debut, Henderson and Klein struck before halftime and Preki found the back of the net in

Above: Meola's sterling season behind a resolute defense brought the opportunity for a title into focus and led him to bargain down from Rolexes to DVD players. Right: Among those in the crowd for the MLS Cup kickoff was Wizards' founder Lamar Hunt, even though his beloved Chiefs were playing their arch-rival Raiders on the same day.

the second half. Chicago trailed 4-1 in the late stages before grabbing two consolation goals, a notable twist that left Vermes and Meola fuming.

"Tony and I were pissed off after that Chicago game," Vermes said. "We vented in the locker room afterwards and told the guys that allowing three goals was unacceptable. We had to be tougher to break down and hungrier for clean sheets. Winning 4-3 wasn't going to cut it. At the end of the day, the team responded well to the message."

Indeed, the Wizards used that moment as a launching point for one of the stingiest defensive runs that MLS has ever seen. Following the Chicago match, three straight shutouts preceded a 2-1 win over the MetroStars. Then, from April 19 to May 27, Kansas City shredded the MLS record books with a 681-minute shutout streak that still stands as the second longest in league history. The unprecedented run produced six straight clean sheets and saw the Wizards score 16 unanswered goals.

"The guiding defensive principle for us was simple," Gansler said. "Defending is like breathing. You always do it."

By the end of May, Kansas City held a comfortable lead atop the standings with 10 wins, zero losses and two draws.

"Sometime very early in the season, I realized, OK, this is doable," Gansler said. "With the group of guys we have, winning a championship is doable."

The Wizards took their first setback on June 4, falling 3-2 to Chicago at Soldier Field. The defeat marked the beginning of a barren stretch in which Kansas City prevailed once in nine matches. Gansler's side weathered the storm, however, and lost only twice in its final 11 games.

Near the end of the Wizards' historic shutout streak, Meola became locked in a bet with three teammates. Going into 2000, the single-season MLS record for most shutouts by a club was 12—a record shared by the 1999 Colorado team that Vermes captained. If the Wizards eclipsed that total, Meola would have to buy Rolex watches for Vermes, Garcia and Prideaux, the three players who had forged a miserly partnership in defense.

By the summertime, it was clear that Kansas City would have a great shot at setting the new shutout record. Unwilling to drop thousands of dollars on Rolex watches, Meola agreed to buy each player a new DVD player instead. Kansas City collected its record-breaking 14th clean sheet with six games to spare.

"Back in 2000, DVDs were hot," Garcia said. "If he had known just how good we were going to be at the start of the season, he never would have thrown Rolexes into that bet."

Ahead of Kansas City's regular season finale at the Tampa Bay Mutiny on Sept. 9, silverware was up for grabs. The MLS Supporters' Shield, a trophy created by MLS supporters groups in 1999, was awarded to the club with the most points. The Wizards sat on 56 points, two points ahead of a Chicago team that visited the Columbus Crew that same night. A victory would guarantee Kansas City the Supporters' Shield, while a draw would open the door for Chicago to move level on points and even win the Shield by virtue of goal difference if it beat Columbus by a three-goal margin.

"In some ways, that game felt like a final," Zavagnin said. "Back then, the Supporters' Shield had yet to catch on as a major honor and wasn't top of mind among fans. But all of us had a sense that we were on the cusp of something incredible, especially after turning things around from 1999. We had the chance to basically go from bottom dweller to the top of the mountain."

The match began ominously for Kansas City, as Tampa Bay took a 2-0 lead in the first half. Three minutes before halftime, the Wizards grabbed a goal back through Chris Henderson on an assist from Vermes. That set the stage for Molnar to notch his team-leading 12th goal of the year in the 66th minute to level the score at 2-2 and give Vermes the first and only multi-assist game of his seven-year MLS career.

"He was a goal-scoring machine, especially in the big games," Gansler said of Molnar, who had nine game-winning goals in 2000. "He had the knack of a goal scorer and the ego of a goal scorer. And that was just what the team needed."

Kansas City emerged with a 2-2 tie and ended the regular season on 57 points, which meant Chicago needed to beat Columbus by at least three goals in order to deny the Wizards the Supporters' Shield. Wizards PR officer Rob Thomson provided Chicago-Columbus score updates from Tampa Bay's stadium locker room as the match finished, and although the Fire would prevail by a 3-2 scoreline, Kansas City had clinched the Supporters' Shield with a plus-two advantage over Chicago in goal differential.

Mo Johnston went head-first to win a 50/50 ball against Galaxy defender Greg Vanney during the "mini game" in the 2000 MLS Cup Playoffs semifinals. Vanny's boot inadvertently caught Johnston above the eye, requiring 18 stitches, but the Scotsman didn't seem to mind as his effort had sprung Miklos Molnar for the match-winning golden goal. The sequence would come to be known by old-school Wizards fans as "The Moment."

The Shield wasn't presented to Kansas City that evening—another indication of the trophy's fledgling status at the time—but the accomplishment was nevertheless significant.

"Finishing first in the league gave us a lift going into the playoffs, for sure," Vermes said. "There's a certain level of confidence you get when you win a trophy. You get more swagger—another notch in your belt—and it makes you stronger mentally. It makes you believe. All of that helps the team in the biggest moments come playoff time."

Later that night in the hotel lobby, Molnar, completely unaware of the MLS playoff system as a longtime player in Europe, announced his retirement. He was ready to go out as a league champion.

"The fact that Miklos planned to retire was made known to us coaches rather quickly," Gansler said. "I remember having a conversation with him and pardon my French, but he pretty much said, 'What the (expletive) is this? There's playoffs?' And so I said, 'Well, in America we do some things differently here.' And he said, 'OK, let's do the double then.'"

Doing the double, of course, required Kansas City to add the MLS Cup to their trophy haul.

THE PINNACLE

The ingredients for a title run were there. Molnar, who had a dozen goals in just 17 matches, was healthy after missing almost half the season through injury. Behind him, Preki recorded a team-best 15 assists and Johnston added four goals and seven assists. Henderson (nine goals, nine assists) and Klein (six goals, eight assists) had been extremely productive on the wings, while McKeon tallied 11 assists as a combative midfielder alongside Zavagnin. Meola posted an astounding 16 shutouts in 31 games, thanks in part to the stellar play of defenders Vermes, Garcia and Prideaux.

The conference semifinals and finals of the 2000 MLS Cup Playoffs featured a unique, first-to-five format. Teams received three points for a win, one for a tie and zero for a loss. The first team to five points over the course of the three-game series advanced.

Kansas City made easy work of Colorado in the quarterfinals, with two home wins bookending a road draw. That set up a tantalizing semifinals showdown with the LA Galaxy, which had reached MLS Cup the previous year and boasted a formidable roster with the likes of U.S. internationals Cobi Jones, Greg Vanney and Robin Fraser as well as Salvadoran talisman Mauricio Cienfuegos and famous Mexican striker Luis Hernandez. Galaxy coach Sigi Schmid was one of the best in the business—a coach Gansler knew quite well.

After the clubs settled for a scoreless draw in Game 1 at Arrowhead Stadium, LA earned a last-gasp 2-1 home win in Game 2 at the Rose Bowl. The result left Kansas City trailing 4-1 on points and needing a victory in Game 3 back home.

"I remember riding to our hotel from the Rose Bowl after Game 2, getting together with Peter and Chris Klein on the bus," Zavagnin said. "There was no doubt in our minds that we were winning Game 3 at Arrowhead. That was just the mentality we had. And sure enough, it ended up being one of the defining games of our season and one of the best I've ever been a part of."

The decisive third match of the semifinals saw 11,815 fans descend on Arrowhead Stadium. The Friday night battle, played amid unseasonably cold temperatures, heated up near the 20th minute when the Wizards were awarded their first penalty kick of the season. Molnar buried the spot kick to give Kansas City a 1-0 lead that stood until the full-time whistle. The result gave both teams four points and set up a sudden death mini-game. If the sides remained tied after 30 minutes, the winner would be decided via penalty shootout.

"The mini-game is one of the biggest and best memories that I have," Garcia said. "As a team, we knew we were going to win. We just didn't know how or when."

Six minutes into the extra frame, Johnston bravely dove to steer a header in behind the defense for Molnar to chase. In doing so, the Scottish forward suffered an inadvertent kick to the head by a Galaxy defender. Racing goalward, Molnar calmly rounded goalkeeper Kevin Hartman and hammered high into the open net for the match-winning golden goal.

The play ignited euphoric celebrations across the stadium—the hit single "Who Let the Dogs Out" by Baha Men blared on the sound system—as several players rushed to embrace Johnston, who beamed with joy as blood rushed down his face. Kansas City was bound for MLS Cup and a date with Chicago on Oct. 15 at RFK Stadium in Washington, D.C.

"That game still gives me goosebumps," Meola said. "The winning goal was an iconic moment that immortalized both Mo and Miklos, but the game itself said so much about the group. I've never seen a team with a stronger defensive mentality. That season, if you didn't score a goal before us, you had no chance to win."

After lifting the championship trophy on the field, players and coaches joined Lamar Hunt in a jaunt to the locker room. Upon arrival, they immediately noticed something missing: no champagne bottles. Stadium staff scrambled around in search of the champagne and soon learned that MLS officials had prematurely placed the bottles in LA's locker room during the second half.

Molnar salutes the crowd at Arrowhead after his winning goal advanced the Wizards to their first-ever MLS Cup.

bar. From there, the Wizards continued to defend in a low block as the Fire attacked in waves. Past the 80th minute, Meola made three impressive stops in quick succession to set an MLS Cup record with 10 saves on the day.

"I've seen my fair share of amazing goalkeeping performances," Vermes said. "I don't think I've seen anything that matched Tony in the MLS Cup. He stood on his head for us all season and that day, he probably won us the game."

With 90 minutes on the clock, fourth official Kevin Stott signaled for a whopping six minutes of stoppage time.

"Those six minutes," Garcia said, "felt like a lifetime."

Flabbergasted, Gansler barked out to referee Paul Tamberino, an official he had long respected and rated highly.

"Six minutes, Paul? Unbelievable! Are you getting paid overtime?"

"This game has been so good," Tamberino slyly responded. "Let's play six more."

In the 96th minute, Tamberino blew his full-time whistle. With a gutsy 1-0 triumph, Kansas City had reached the pinnacle as MLS Cup champions just one year after finishing in last place. The club's meteoric rise, sprawled across an entire storybook season, had ended in glory.

"That game and that season showed that when you have a hungry group of guys like that, it doesn't matter how good the individuals are," Vermes said. "It matters what the collective group can do."

After hoisting the Alan I. Rothenberg trophy on the field, the Wizards reveled in locker room champagne showers. Molnar retired for the second time. Uche Okafor and Alex Bunbury announced the ends of their careers. Johnston also declared his retirement, although he wound up returning for one final season in 2001.

The MLS Cup champions then returned to their D.C. hotel. Fresh off his 21st shutout of the season including playoffs, Meola received a phone call from his cousin. Meola's father was incredibly proud of his son, but he was also exhausted. The family had already begun their drive back home to New Jersey.

Not long later—as players, coaches and club staff carried their celebrations into a banquet hall—Meola and Gansler engaged in a private conversation.

"At the start of the season, I told you I would trade you back to New York," Gansler told Meola. "So I'm going to do that. I'm a man of my word."

Meola paused for a second and looked at Gansler. "Thanks, Bob, but I don't think you need to do that. I want to stay in Kansas City."

For the next four years, KC was Meola's home.

There were no citywide celebrations or trips to the White House, but the victory did get the Wizards onto a cereal box. A few months after the MLS Cup triumph, Kellogg's Frosted Flakes distributed a limited-edition series of boxes honoring the Wizards championship, with Meola, Garcia and Henderson prominently featured on the cover. It was a telltale sign that Kansas City had accomplished something special that resonated nationally.

"We definitely didn't come back to a tickertape parade after winning the cup because there wasn't all that much local fanfare," Garcia said. "But for those who believed in us and were true fans, it was such a special time. To see the team appear on Frosted Flakes—that was the 'wow' moment for me."

Although the team had yet to gain legitimate traction in the Kansas City region, Gansler and the Wizards had delivered the city and shown just how quickly a club's fortunes could be altered in MLS. ♦

There would be no parade in Kansas City or visit to the White House, but the 2000 MLS Champions had the MLS Cup—and a cereal box—to add to their trophy case.

MLS CUP
CHAMPIONS

AQUAFINA
EPER OF THE YEAR

PEPSI BEST 11
2000
TONY MEOLA
GOALKEEPER
KANSAS CITY WIZARDS

HONDA

HONDA
2000 Honda Most Valuable Player
TONY MEOLA
Kansas City Wizards

MLS
2000

MY STORY: TONY MEOLA

When you talk about changes in life, sometime changes are scary. The move to Kansas City was scary for me, but it turned out to be the best change the I've ever experienced in my life.

My first season in Kansas City in 1999 didn't go well. I got injured on St. Patrick's Day, and my season was essentially over. At that point I was thinking that I had to do everything I could to get out of Kansas City and back to the East Coast. I mean I got hurt in this place, we finished in last place, my friend Alexi Lalas—who I had been traded here with—had just retired.

But then Bob Gansler came in as the new coach, and as I was having conversations with Bob, he asked me to stick it out and go through the offseason and figure things out. He said if I would give him one year, he would give me a new contract and then after the one year, he would trade me back to the East Coast. Obviously, I didn't play the year before in 1999, and Bob was planning on bringing in a bunch of guys that I knew, so I thought this sounded like a good plan. And as people know, you don't really say "no" to Bob Gansler that easily.

I realized pretty much from the start of the 2000 season that I was a fan favorite here in KC. The fans were just great. We didn't have a lot of superstars in that group. It was more like a team of misfits. We had a bunch of guys who came here from other places where people didn't want us.

I remember after the first game of that season when we beat Chicago, somebody turned on loud music, and it happened to be the song "Who Let the Dogs Out?" We had just won 4-3, it was kind of a crazy game, and Chicago was the team that everybody was gunning for. That song became sort of an anthem for our team for the entire season, and we played it all the time!

You can say what you want about Kansas City back then and the team maybe not having the kind of resources that they do now, but things were changing, and Lamar Hunt started treating us and the Chiefs players like equals. They moved us from Swope Park into the Arrowhead practice facility, and we got treated great—we had everything we needed.

Right after we won the 2000 MLS Cup, we had a celebration at the team hotel with our families, and during that Bob pulled me into a corner with Lamar Hunt and said "Look, I made a promise to you. I told you I would get you back home, and I'm going to get you back." I told him that I didn't want to leave Kansas City. I don't know if I had thought about it until that second, but I knew that my wife was enjoying being here, the people were wonderful and the organization was great. From what I could tell, I think Bob kind of knew that I was going to say that because of how things went that season, but I'll never forget that Bob Gansler was true to his word.

I have great memories of playing in Kansas City. One thing that stands out was that the amount of media coverage of the Wizards. When I was in New York, there were times where we had played a game, and you couldn't find any coverage, or maybe there was a little blurb in one of the newspapers. But in Kansas City, everything we did was publicized, everything we did was on the news. I spent a lot of time back then on Metro Sports with Dave Stewart—they gave us a ton of coverage—and I also had a weekly radio show on Sports Radio 810. Things like that wouldn't have happened in New York. There was nothing that happened with the Wizards that wasn't publicized, which was really cool.

I also think that the level of competition back then is comparable to Major League Soccer today, and with only 10-12 teams, some of the rosters were just loaded. Bruce Arena will tell you that those D.C. United teams back then could go up against any team in the league today. I'm proud of how far MLS has come, but I know that the top teams back in my day could still compete today.

2000 MLS Cup
2000 Supporters' Shield
2004 U.S. Open Cup

Tony Meola represented the United States at the 1990, 1994 and 2002 FIFA World Cups. In 2000, Meola was named MLS MVP, Goalkeeper of the Year and MLS Cup MVP as he led the Wizards to the 2000 MLS Cup Championship. Meola was also named to the MLS All-Time Best XI team and was inducted into the National Soccer Hall of Fame in 2012.

SNAPSHOT
WIZARDS
1997-2010

1) Wizards pennant, circa 1997.

2) Preki's cleats, autographed.

3) Tony Meola's goalkeeper gloves, 2000 season, autographed

4) Head Coach Bob Gansler's polo, MLS Cup 2000.

5) Midfielder Chris Klein's autographed match-worn jersey, MLS Cup 2000.

6) Autographed Wizards team photo, taken at the brand-new elephant exhibit at the Kansas City Zoo, 1999 (featuring seven World Cup veterans and four National Soccer Hall of Fame members).

7) MLS Cup 2000 matchball, autographed by entire team.

8) "Building Soccer" brochure, promoting the new "Kansas City Soccer Stadium," 2010.

1

2

3

4

5

1999 KANSAS CITY WIZARDS™
Front row (L to R): Chris Henderson, Brian Johnson, Mo Johnston, Preki Radosavljevic, Digital Takawira, Vicente Figueroa, Jesse Van Saun, Nino Da Silva
Middle row (L to R): Rob Thomson (Public Relations), Joey Becera (Team Administration), Jake Dancy, Scott Uderitz, Ken Fogarty (Asst. Coach), Bob Gansler (Head Coach), Alan Mayer (Goalkeeper Coach), Alex Bunbury, Scott Vermillion, Francisco Gomez, Gary Minnick (Equipment Manager), Chet North (Trainer)
Back row (L to R): Tony Soto, Chris Klein, Brandon Prideaux, Alexi Lalas, Tony Meola, Chris Snitko, Uche Okafor, Sean Bowers, Michael Green, Chris Brown
© 1999 MLS TM
Photo by Scott Indermaur
Photo Location - Kansas City Zoo

CARONDELET HEALTH
St. Mary's Hospital of Blue Springs System
Saint Joseph Health System

MLS

6

Mitre
MLS
ULTIMAX
MAJOR LEAGUE SOCCER

7

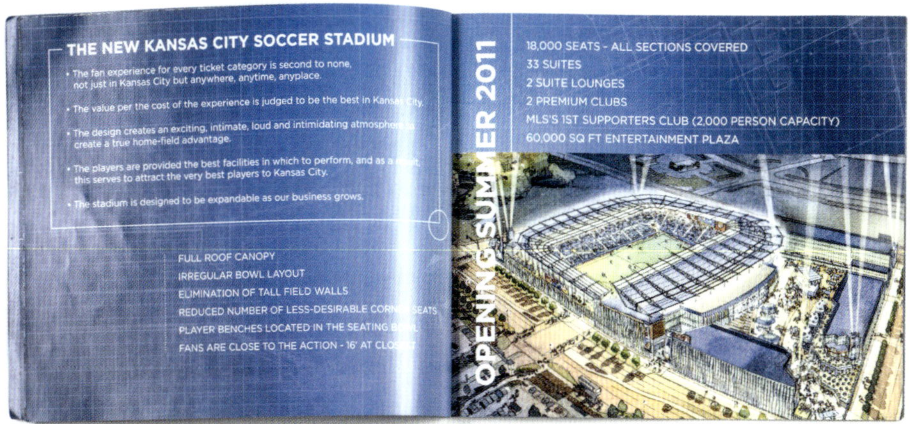
THE NEW KANSAS CITY SOCCER STADIUM
The fan experience for every ticket category is second to none, not just in Kansas City but anywhere, anytime, anyplace.
The value per the cost of the experience is judged to be the best in Kansas City.
The design creates an exciting, intimate, loud and intimidating atmosphere to create a true home-field advantage.
The players are provided the best facilities in which to perform, and as a result, this serves to attract the very best players to Kansas City.
The stadium is designed to be expandable as our business grows.
FULL ROOF CANOPY
IRREGULAR BOWL LAYOUT
ELIMINATION OF TALL FIELD WALLS
REDUCED NUMBER OF LESS-DESIRABLE CORNER SEATS
PLAYER BENCHES LOCATED IN THE SEATING BOWL
FANS ARE CLOSE TO THE ACTION - 16' AT CLOSEST
OPENING SUMMER 2011
18,000 SEATS - ALL SECTIONS COVERED
33 SUITES
2 SUITE LOUNGES
2 PREMIUM CLUBS
MLS'S 1ST SUPPORTERS CLUB (2,000 PERSON CAPACITY)
60,000 SQ FT ENTERTAINMENT PLAZA

8

Wizards midfielder Sasha Victorine wins a header on a corner kick against the Houston Dynamo in front of an announced crowd of 8,196.

NO SURRENDER

HOW KANSAS CITY SAVED ITS SOCCER CLUB

Major League Soccer in Kansas City was on life support. Though the Wizards had won an MLS title in 2000, the victory didn't do much to establish the team in the city it called home. The league was struggling as well. It dropped to 10 teams in 2002, and for a time the next year, two owners—soccer patriarch Lamar Hunt and billionaire Philip Anschutz—were operating nine of the 10 clubs.

"We heard whispers that the league was not on solid footing," said Wizards midfielder Kerry Zavagnin. "And Kansas City was probably the most unsettling market or one of the most unsettling markets in a league that was trying to establish itself."

Indeed, one of the defining characteristics of the early years of MLS was sparse crowds, especially in Kansas City. Most lasting memories of the inaugural Wiz/Wizards era seem to focus not on the successes on the field or the big-name players such as Preki, Tony Meola or Alexi Lalas, but rather on the relative emptiness of cavernous Arrowhead Stadium, scattered with crowds of screaming 12-year-olds and plastic noisemakers. In three of the first five seasons of MLS, the Wizards finished last in attendance. Even high-water mark matches saw Arrowhead's lower bowl half-empty.

Even for major matches like the 2004 U.S. Open Cup Final, Arrowhead remained largely empty.

"We were tenants," said Zavagnin. "Playing second fiddle to the real tenants at Arrowhead. So to not have a real home ... we didn't have an identity."

Hunt had worked tirelessly to keep the Wizards alive and build a following, taking star goalkeeper Meola around the city to drum up interest prior to the 2003 season. It worked to the tune of over 6,000 season tickets sold, but it was a stopgap at best. After the season ended, the Hunt family ownership group called a meeting of the entire club staff, including the players and coaches. They told them they were considering putting the franchise up for sale.

"It took the wind out of our sails initially ... when you find out that an ownership group doesn't want you anymore," said Wizards defender Jimmy Conrad. "But there was no drop off from the Hunts at all. I mean, they still cared. They still wanted to make it work. Lamar Hunt was cold-calling people saying, 'Hey, I'm Lamar Hunt. You want to buy some Wizards tickets?' And I think he probably had a 100 percent sales rate because he's Lamar Hunt."

Though the 2004 season saw tremendous success on the field—the Wizards won their first U.S. Open Cup, missed out on the Supporters' Shield on the fourth tiebreakier and made it to the MLS Cup finals—the business picture hadn't changed. Despite the efforts of the Hunt family and others to raise the status of the Club in the community, the Wizards were faltering financially. Season ticket sales and overall attendance both declined in 2004. Discount tickets seemed to always be available—often for less than $5—and most, if not all, of the Wizards corporate sponsors had agreed to the deal as throw-away add-ons to much larger partnership agreements with the Chiefs.

The Wizards had a small, rabid fanbase, but the club's identity had not taken hold in the city. On Dec. 9, 2004, less than a month after the heartbreaking loss in MLS Cup final, Lamar Hunt held a press conference and made it official: The Kansas City Wizards were on the market.

In the immediate aftermath of Hunt's announcement, the lack of major public uproar was perhaps the most telling indicator of the club's status in the city. It was picked up by a few national news publications, but didn't even warrant a feature story in the Sports Business Journal, the news instead relegated to the "Closing Bell" daily recap.

"It wasn't like there was this outcry outside of a few thousand people who were trying to save the Wizards," said Zavagnin. "We were what? Nine years as a club in our history? It wasn't on the news. Social media was nonexistent at the time. So the sharing of the platform was probably BigSoccer."

BigSoccer.com was the preeminent American soccer internet community in the early-2000s, providing fans all over the country with an internet message board to share news and opinions. Which meant it was still a fledgling niche within a niche. The Kansas City Wizards forum, however, was one of the more trafficked communities on the site, boasting several hundred consistent visitors. A fairly large number of those were regular participants, and a couple dozen active super-users interacted on an everyday basis. It was people in this group who initially decided they were going to "Save the Wizards."

Within an hour of Hunt's announcement, the small, passionate internet community had begun to mobilize. While the mood on the board was somber and the situation seemed dire, the consensus was they weren't going down without a fight. Derek Gathright, a 24-year-old fan who came of age with the team, posted the first "Help Save The Wizards" thread. His manifesto argued, in part, "we need to do everything we can to preserve our passion. This thread will be dedicated to ideas, discussion, and hopefully the eventual news that our team is staying … we aren't going to get a second chance." And soon, an ad hoc groundswell began of people who were prepared to fight to keep the team in Kansas City.

"I was terrified of never seeing an MLS team in Kansas City again," said Gathright. "We all were. One of my favorite things in the world was about to be taken from me. What was the risk? Failure? That pales in comparison to the lifelong regret of 'I did nothing to stop it.'"

They soon moved from an internet text thread to a formal organization. The Heart of America Soccer Foundation was officially formed on Dec. 12 in a boardroom at a downtown Kansas City, Missouri, law office. The initial meeting was attended by 20 to 30 Kansas Citians from all walks of life: lawyers, architects, bartenders, college students, Wizards staffers, multigenerational families. All ilk of soccer fans were seemingly represented (later meetings would include special guests, business leaders, and current and former Wizards players). Much of the group was made up of members of the Mystics, the club's small, unofficial supporters' group and the precursor to the modern-day Cauldron.

"The Mystics at the time was a small handful of rabid fans, who were, let's face it, a bit socially awkward," said Gathright. "'Hello, stranger. I love soccer, but I have no friends who like soccer, so in a sea of 70,000 empty seats I want to watch the games with you.' And over time, those strangers became friends, who became family. When faced with your family being taken from you, the natural reaction is to fight for it. HASF was that natural reaction."

What began as a web post was soon a full-fledged nonprofit organization. Websites were created, flyers were printed, stickers were stuck, and a mission statement was drafted. From the

The HASF website listed the group's vision and mission, including the statement, "We believe the Kansas City Wizards are a tremendous asset and are dedicated to finding a permanent solution to keep them in Kansas City.

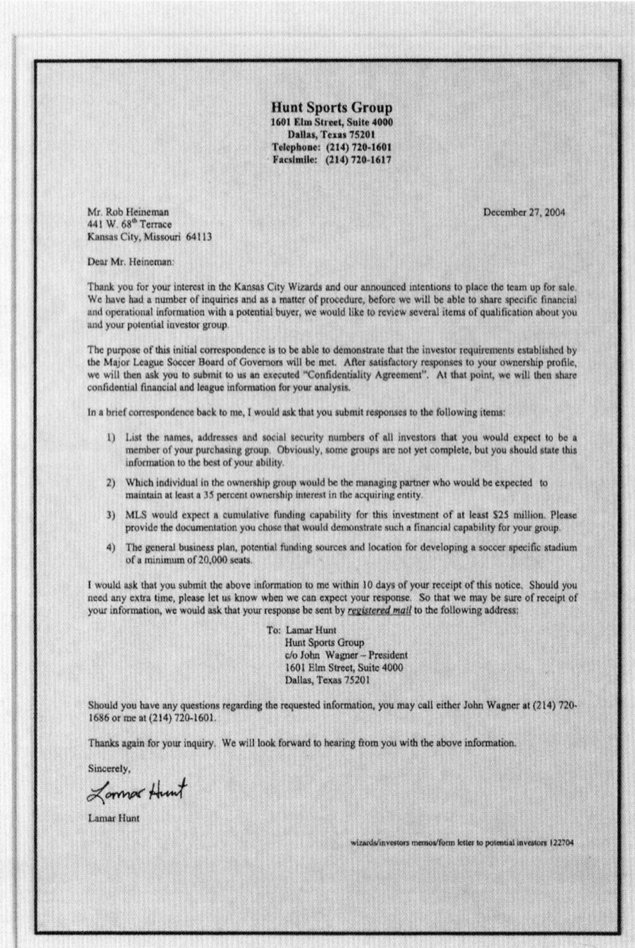

Hunt Sports Group
1601 Elm Street, Suite 4000
Dallas, Texas 75201
Telephone: (214) 720-1601
Facsimile: (214) 720-1617

Mr. Rob Heineman
441 W. 68th Terrace
Kansas City, Missouri 64113

December 27, 2004

Dear Mr. Heineman:

Thank you for your interest in the Kansas City Wizards and our announced intentions to place the team up for sale. We have had a number of inquiries and as a matter of procedure, before we will be able to share specific financial and operational information with a potential buyer, we would like to review several items of qualification about you and your potential investor group.

The purpose of this initial correspondence is to be able to demonstrate that the investor requirements established by the Major League Soccer Board of Governors will be met. After satisfactory responses to your ownership profile, we will then ask you to submit to us an executed "Confidentiality Agreement". At that point, we will then share confidential financial and league information for your analysis.

In a brief correspondence back to me, I would ask that you submit responses to the following items:

1) List the names, addresses and social security numbers of all investors that you would expect to be a member of your purchasing group. Obviously, some groups are not yet complete, but you should state this information to the best of your ability.
2) Which individual in the ownership group would be the managing partner who would be expected to maintain at least a 35 percent ownership interest in the acquiring entity.
3) MLS would expect a cumulative funding capability for this investment of at least $25 million. Please provide the documentation you chose that would demonstrate such a financial capability for your group.
4) The general business plan, potential funding sources and location for developing a soccer specific stadium of a minimum of 20,000 seats.

I would ask that you submit the above information to me within 10 days of your receipt of this notice. Should you need any extra time, please let us know when we can expect your response. So that we may be sure of receipt of your information, we would ask that your response be sent by *registered mail* to the following address:

To: Lamar Hunt
Hunt Sports Group
c/o John Wagner – President
1601 Elm Street, Suite 4000
Dallas, Texas 75201

Should you have any questions regarding the requested information, you may call either John Wagner at (214) 720-1686 or me at (214) 720-1601.

Thanks again for your inquiry. We will look forward to hearing from you with the above information.

Sincerely,

Lamar Hunt

Lamar Hunt

wizards/investors memos/form letter to potential investors 122704

Lamar Hunt's letter, addressed to Heineman on Dec. 27, 2004, thanking him for his group's interest in purchasing the Wizards and listing the requirements for ownership and the next steps in the process.

beginning, it was clear to all involved that simply finding an owner wasn't going to "Save the Wizards." It would take changing the culture around the sport in the city. It needed to be more than an occasional fun weekend diversion for the casual soccer family. The diehard fans were hoping to convince the entire city that a soccer team could become part of the city's identity, in the same way that the football and baseball teams had historically been.

For Kansas City's soccer team to survive and thrive, it needed a stadium, a fan experience and a culture all its own. Without it, they were going to lose their team.

"I think San Antonio was a destination [the league] was discussing, among others. And I thought that would have been a shame, given what Kansas City is and where it is on the map," said Conrad. "You could sense that there was, you know, a bubbling fandom. Obviously, you could see it with the Chiefs and the Royals ... and because there was no NBA or NHL, there was definitely room for it ... you just had to open a facility that was specific to that and speaking to that."

In his search for a suitable owner to take over the Wizards in Kansas City, Hunt reached out to Kevin Gray, President of the Kansas City Sports Commission. Gray was instrumental in just about anything that happened in sports in the city during the early 2000s, including Kansas Speedway and Sprint Center. Hunt and Gray had worked alongside one another in the past, while Hunt was exploring potential soccer stadium complexes for the Wizards, and that was how they had first been introduced to Robb Heineman and Greg Maday.

Heineman and Maday owned a private equity investment firm and were interested in the retail development at Hunt's rumored soccer complex. Heineman's family had experience in professional sports with their investment in a minor league basketball team, but neither of them was a big soccer fan or had even been to a Wizards game until late in the 2003 season when Hunt invited Heineman to a match to discuss the complex.

In those early conversations, Hunt explained his belief that soccer-specific stadiums were the future of MLS, comparing it to how the NFL hadn't exploded until they moved away from multipurpose stadiums and into football-only venues where they were fully able to control the fan experience.

In early December, Hunt called them for a meeting at Arrowhead and explained that he was officially putting the team up for sale and hoped that they might be interested in making a bid.

"We feel like we've got everything you need to try and make this happen," they told Hunt, "other than the money, the political capital and the know-how. Other than that, we've got it whipped. But, hey— super interested."

Hunt had been clear at his announcement that his preference was for the team to stay in Kansas City. But he was equally clear that he would only sell the team to a local bidder if there was a stadium plan in place. The stadium was the key to everything. Unfortunately, it was also the biggest hurdle. Building a sports venue requires capital, public interest, available land and a willing municipal partner. Kansas City was lacking for most, if not all.

As the 2005 season kicked off with a cloud of

uncertainty hanging over it, Wizards coach Bob Gansler was retooling the roster for a new generation. A shock loss to the lower-division Minnesota Thunder ended the team's U.S. Open Cup title defense in the quarterfinals, and was the beginning of a nine-match winless streak in all competitions. An away draw at FC Dallas on the final day of the season sealed their fate, and the Wizards missed the playoffs by two points.

Off the field, things weren't progressing as quickly as anybody would have liked on the ownership front. Heineman and Maday had formed a small group interested in purchasing the team called KCS Acquisitions Group consisting of investors they had worked with extensively: C3 Holdings founder Pat Curran and David French, another partner in their private equity firm Rock Island Capital. In late spring 2005, word began to leak out there was a potential local ownership group interested in buying the Wizards, but they stayed anonymous and behind the scenes.

Meanwhile the public messaging from Gray at the Sports Commission, Commissioner Don Garber at MLS and the fans in HASF was clear: There was a path to keeping the team in Kansas City, but it was going to take public incentives from a city or state to help develop a stadium.

True to the conversations with Hunt, KCS was convinced a dedicated stadium plan was the key to success in American soccer and in Kansas City. That meant they needed more investors and more capital if their ownership bid was going to be successful.

As it happened, 2005 became a year of growth for the league. MLS was in the second year of a landmark new partnership with adidas, two new clubs expanded the league's number to 12 teams, and Soccer United Marketing, a joint-venture between MLS and U.S. Soccer, owned the television rights to broadcast the 2010 and 2014 World Cups in the United States. The value of MLS was growing, almost daily. The question became whether an ownership group that could keep the team in Kansas City would coalesce in time to save the Wizards. (Longtime Kansas City sports fans were still smarting over the departure of the NBA Kings to Sacramento in 1985, right at the dawn of the Michael Jordan-fueled explosion in popularity that pro basketball would enjoy in the coming decades.)

Throughout 2005 and early 2006, HASF continued to hold events and drum up awareness for the team, its members' enthusiasm waxing and waning with every new rumor or piece of news. Over the course of that early two-year period, the deal to purchase the team died and rose from the dead at least half a dozen times.

"That group (HASF) kept it in our mind and in our face so we'd pay attention to it," said Heineman.

In the meantime, more and more North Ameri-

A scattered crowd of 8,710 looks on as Wizards goalkeeper Will Hesmer watches a shot carom off the crossbar during the June 28, 2006, match against D.C. United.

can cities were expressing interest in MLS franchises, and the league was starting to expand at a steady pace, creating a sense of urgency. After Chivas USA (Los Angeles) and Real Salt Lake joined the league in 2005, Houston, Philadelphia and Toronto were rumored to be next in line.

The league's focus seemed to be on Philadelphia, and when MLS Commissioner Don Garber visited Kansas City near the end of the 2005 season, he made it clear to the players on the team that unless something came together quickly, they should all be prepared to move.

"When the commissioner comes to your city, sits you down and says, 'could be Philadelphia, could be Houston,' the possibility of that relocation becomes very real," said Zavagnin.

Kansas City had work to do, and fast. Heineman, Maday and their KCS group still needed to find additional local investors with pockets deep enough to own the team the right way.

Then they had an idea. At a KCS board meeting one day, discussing the soccer project, Maday said, "You know, I'm on the board of the American Royal with Neal Patterson. Maybe I should talk to him about getting involved in what we're doing."

Patterson, alongside his partner Cliff Illig and others, had founded medical technology giant Cerner Corporation on a bench in Kansas City's Loose Park in the 1970s, and turned it into a mulitbillion-dollar business. Maday took their pitch regarding the Wizards to Patterson, who passed it along to Illig, the more analytical of the pair.

Illig met them at their offices on the Country Club Plaza for their first session of discussions about the opportunity. Armed with his customary notepad and blue pen, Illig took "a million notes" over the course of several hours. As they wrapped up, he looked at the group and said succinctly, "I really think it makes sense for us to dig into this."

An important next step was to arrange a trip for the whole contingent, KCS plus Patterson and Illig, to go to Dallas to see the new soccer-specific stadium for Hunt's Dallas MLS entry, then under construction in suburban Frisco.

It would turn out to be one of the most consequential trips in Kansas City sports history. On the flight, Patterson and Illig examined the financial numbers of the team and the league, and the group talked about the outline of a potential partnership.

After they toured the stadium and were readying to return to Kansas City, Patterson asked the big questions: Did they all want to come together and buy the team? And what would each of them bring to the group? On the flight back, they put together the concept, and the construct of the partnership came together.

The group had taken shape, but Patterson and Illig were still not entirely convinced the investment was sound. Soccer in America had a long way to go, and Kansas City hadn't exactly proven its mettle. It was far from a safe bet.

Once again, Lamar Hunt closed the sale. Over a dinner at Capital Grille on the Country Club Plaza, Hunt made his final pitch to Patterson and Illig, who as the potential large-equity investors ultimately held the keys. Hunt didn't talk much about the economics of the deal or the future of soccer. Instead, he focused on civic pride.

"My dad knew a couple things about them," Clark Hunt told *Kansas City Star* in 2019. "They had

Fans hung signs along the front-row railing at Arrowhead Stadium showing their support.

the financial resources to make it work over the long haul, and they were very engaged in Kansas City and doing things that were good for Kansas City. In my dad's mind, that probably made them perfect."

The pitch was simple: Part of what made Kansas City "major league" was its sports teams. Losing one of them, even one that hadn't yet established a foothold, risked that major league status. And if soccer in America was headed where Hunt thought it was, Kansas City couldn't be on the outside looking in. It was too important. Kansas City couldn't afford to lose this team.

"It would be great," Hunt told them, "if you could steward this for me on a go-forward basis."

After saying their goodbyes to Hunt that night and leaving the restaurant, Patterson looked at Illig and asked, "Are we going to do this?"

"I don't think we have any choice," said Illig.

OnGoal, LLC was incorporated in May 2006, with the intent of purchasing the Wizards from the Hunt family. The group consisted of majority owners Patterson and Illig, alongside Maday, Curran, Heineman and French. But the sale of a sports franchise can be like turning a cruise ship: slow, stilted and fighting the current. In this case, even though the ownership group was coming together, there was a growing interest on the part of other cities to avoid the increasingly competitive MLS expansion process and simply buy the Wizards and move them to another city. The league seemed to believe the most likely outcome would see the team moving to Philadelphia.

Late one night in July after an Open Cup game at the Blue Valley District Activities Complex, Heineman called the Commissioner from the parking lot. He told Garber he believed they finally had the right group together to buy the team.

"No, it's going to go to Philadelphia."

"No, I think we've really got a group."

Above, the Heart of America Soccer Foundation papered the city's soccer complexes with stickers and flyers and held fundraising tailgates before Wizards matches.

As the sun set and the lot emptied, Heineman sat in his car in the dark, walking the Commissioner through the makeup of the ownership group, highlighting Patterson and Illig's contributions, and discussing the finer deal points.

Garber negotiated with them all the way up to the end of August, but finally, in the nick of time, the deed was done.

On Aug. 30, 2006, the Wizards played the New York Red Bulls to a 2-2 draw at Arrowhead, thanks to a second-half equalizer from Josh Wolff. But upstairs in Lamar Hunt's owners' suite, a celebration was taking place. Very few of the 6,103 in attendance knew that the most important result in Kansas City soccer history had happened earlier in the day: Hunt and his family had signed the paperwork to sell the Kansas City Wizards to OnGoal, LLC.

The deal was announced the next day in Overland Park, Kansas, at a press conference focused on the legacy of sports and the potential for soccer in Kansas City. Much was made of plans for a future stadium in south Johnson County, Kansas. But that was all discussion for the future. For now what mattered was the team wasn't leaving. Kansas City had saved the Wizards.

"We are especially pleased to have been able to consummate this transaction with the end result that the Wizards will remain in the Kansas City Metropolitan Area," Hunt's announcement said. "We had numerous inquiries from potential investors who wanted to move the team to other communities. Fortunately, the leadership of OnGoal has a passion for the Heart of America, and I am convinced that they will achieve the much-needed soccer-specific stadium for the area and contribute to the long-range success of MLS."

Hunt would pass away on Dec. 13, 2006, 104 days after the sale of the team. He had battled prostate cancer since 1998, but had rarely let it slow him down. Just one month before his death, he had stood on the field at Pizza Hut Park in Dallas, as his new soccer stadium complex hosted MLS Cup 2006.

"Lamar was about as happy as we've ever seen him, even after the game, walking on the field with a big smile on his face," said Garber.

He never got to see his plans about soccer in Kansas City come to fruition, but he seemed comfortable knowing he had left it in visionary hands. "The final story of the 'success' of Major League Soccer has yet to be written. In my opinion it is well on the way and certain to come," Hunt said in his announcement of the sale.

The success wouldn't happen overnight. It had taken 18 months to sell the team, and it would take nearly five years more before Kansas City would have a soccer stadium to call its own, but in the moment, it didn't matter. Thanks to the hard work and efforts of the Hunt Family organization, the KC Sports Commission, Patterson, Illig, Maday, Curran, Heineman and the fans in the Heart of America Soccer Foundation, the team was staying in KC.

Now, for the new owners, it was time to learn from the hard lessons of the past, and plot a path forward toward making Kansas City's soccer team an integral part of the city.

"We couldn't spell soccer when we bought the team," Illig joked to Sam Mellinger of the *Kansas City Star* in 2019. But the owners knew if they were to be successful, they needed to approach this problem the way they had their entire careers: attacking it from every angle and sweating every detail.

That also meant having a clear picture of what they wanted the club to become. Their vision—which they defined as "a vivid description of a future state"—was simple, but audacious: build the best and most innovative soccer specific stadium in the country, with the finest atmosphere and fan experience. And turn a small fanbase built on the backs of youth soccer teams and a smattering of diehards into one of the most rabid and bought-in supporters cultures in the league.

Luckily, it was a dream echoed by the supporters who, for 10 years, had followed the team through thick and thin, and had fought so hard to keep their club in Kansas City.

"We never wanted HASF to solely be focused on selling the team. That purpose was too narrow," said Gathright. "Even after that (hopefully) occurred, there was a lot of work that would be needed to ensure the team didn't turn out to be Wizards 2.0. The broader vision was that Kansas City could become a flagship for soccer and fandom in the United States."

The heavy lifting was just beginning. ♦

Opposite: The OnGoal ownership group at the sale announcement, Aug. 31, 2006; from left to right: David French, Pat Curran, Neal Patterson, Cliff Illig, Robb Heineman and Greg Maday.

WIZARDS
adidas

SNAPSHOT
SUMMER OF SOCCER
2010

The summer of 2010 changed the game of soccer in Kansas City forever.

It began modestly, with about 200 fans at the USA's group-stage World Cup opener vs. England, hosted by the Wizards at the Power & Light District. But by the end of the U.S. run in the tournament, capacity crowds of 12,000 were filling the "Living Room," and the watch parties were generating national attention.

On the heels of the watch parties, the Wizards announced the biggest match in Kansas City history: English powerhouse Manchester United coming to Arrowhead to face the Wizards. Season ticket holders got the first shot at tickets for the game, and the day they went on sale the club sold 1,600 new season tickets for the 2011 season, which would open at the new stadium.

The summer was capped by the biggest celebration of all, as the Wizards earned the upset in front of a record crowd, many of whom had started cheering for the team in red and wound up rooting for the team in blue.

"It was the tipping point," said Peter Vermes afterward. "It woke people up to us. And I guess I'm 1-0 versus Sir Alex Ferguson.

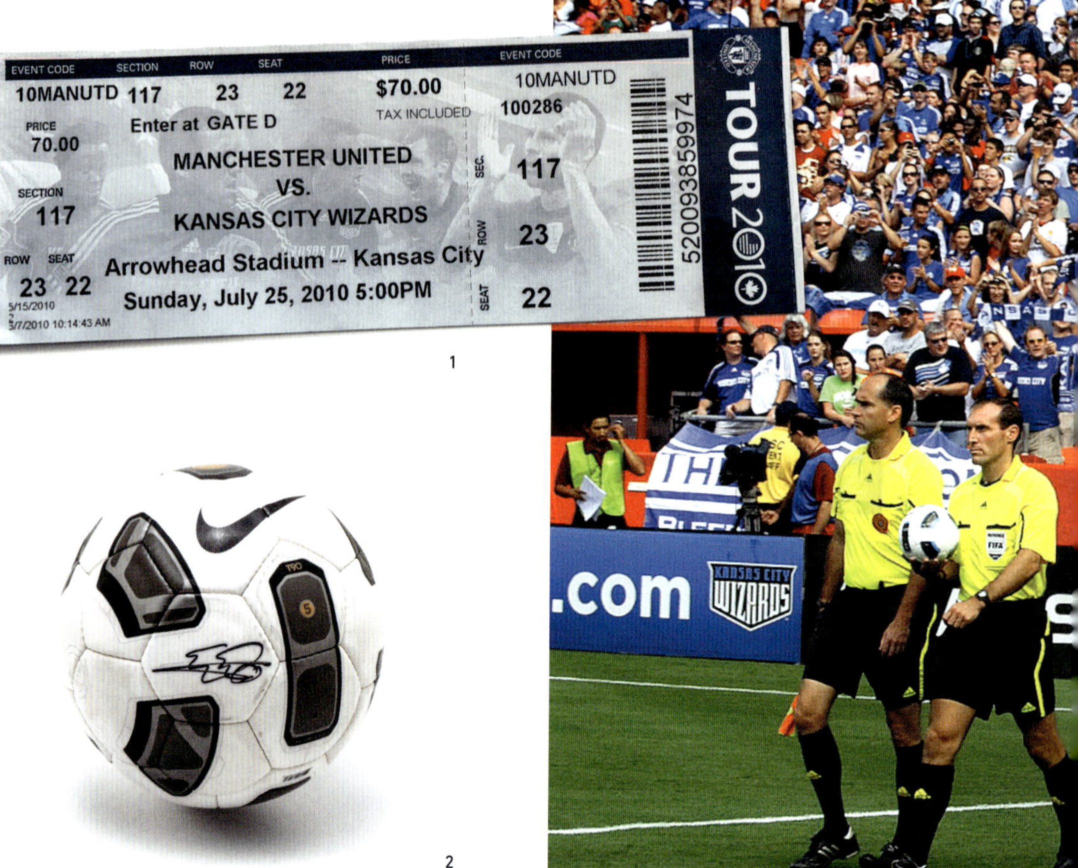

1

2

1) Ticket stub, KC Wizards vs. Manchester United.

2) KCW/Man Utd match ball autographed by Edwin van der Sar.

3) Captains Ryan Giggs and Davy Arnaud lead their teams onto the field, July 25, 2010, in front of 52,424 fans.

4) A capacity crowd of more than 12,000 watched the United States against Ghana at Power & Light District.

5) "Summer of Soccer" World Cup Watch Party promo poster.

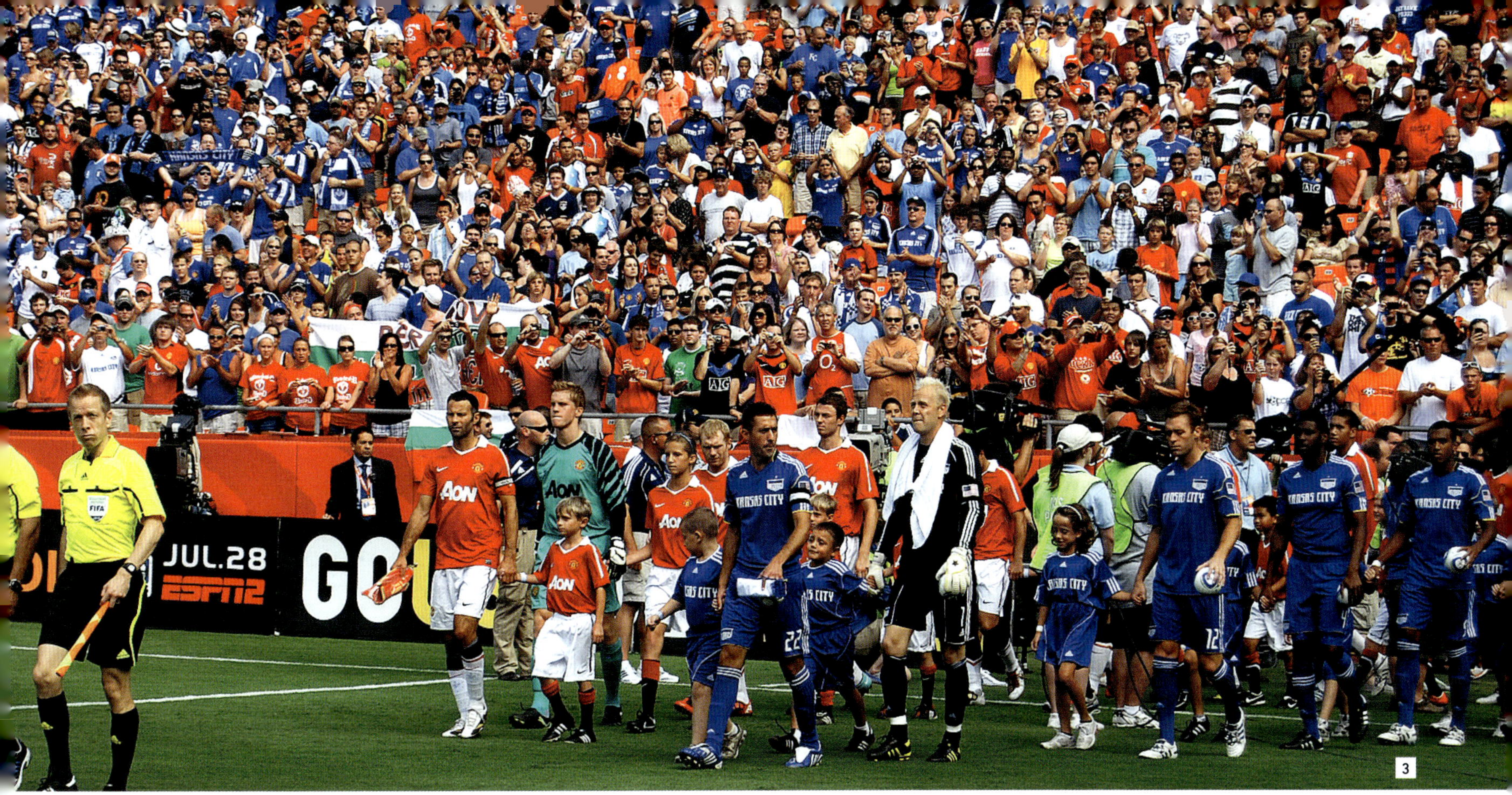

3

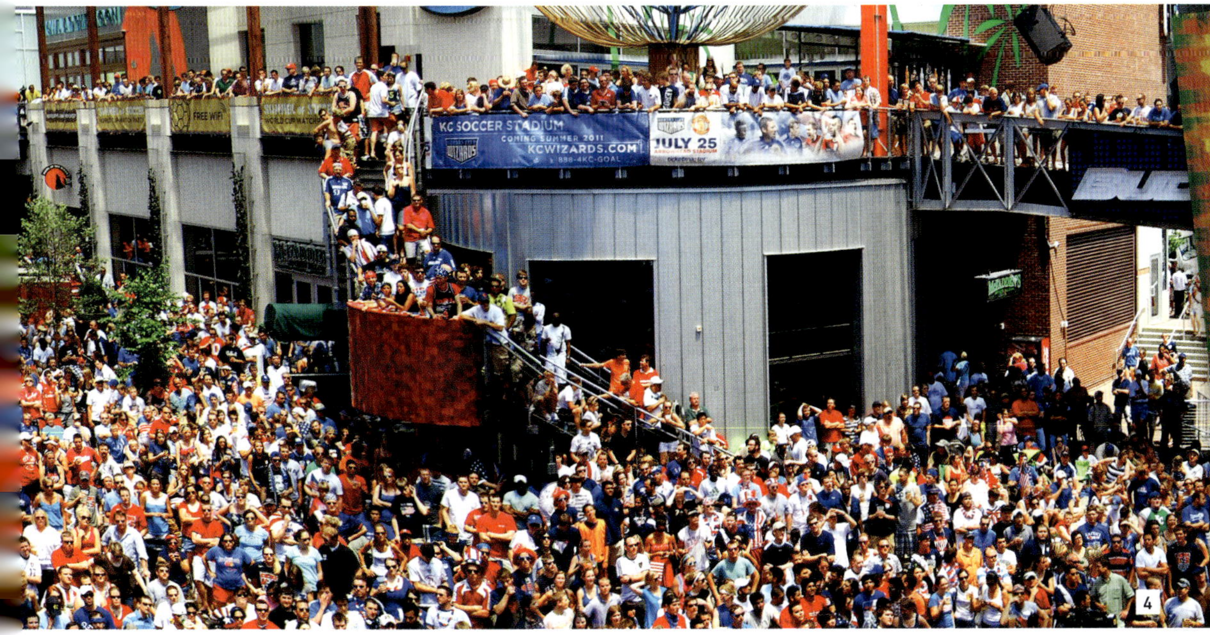

4

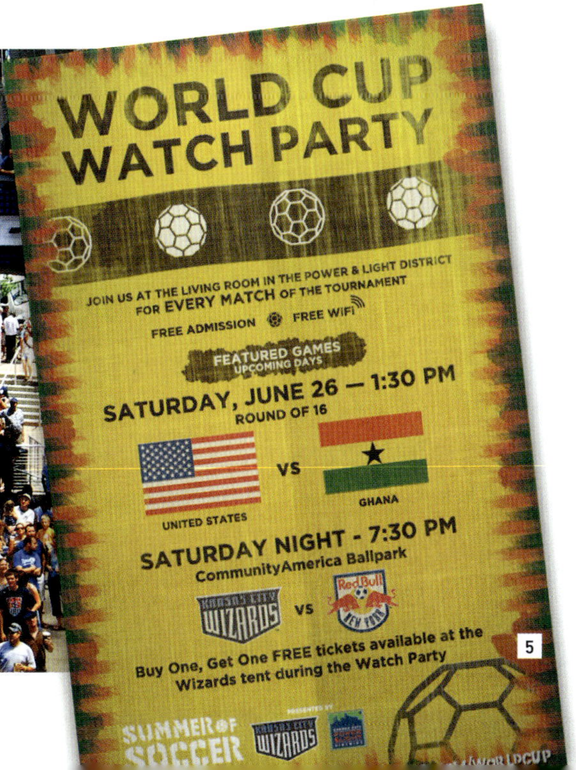

WORLD CUP WATCH PARTY

JOIN US AT THE LIVING ROOM IN THE POWER & LIGHT DISTRICT FOR EVERY MATCH OF THE TOURNAMENT

FREE ADMISSION · FREE WiFi

FEATURED GAMES
UPCOMING DAYS

SATURDAY, JUNE 26 — 1:30 PM
ROUND OF 16

UNITED STATES VS GHANA

SATURDAY NIGHT - 7:30 PM
CommunityAmerica Ballpark

WIZARDS VS NEW YORK

Buy One, Get One FREE tickets available at the Wizards tent during the Watch Party

SUMMER OF SOCCER · WIZARDS

5

adidas
KANSAS CITY
WIZARDS
WIZARDS

MY STORY: JIMMY CONRAD

2004 U.S. Open Cup

Jimmy Conrad was the 2005 MLS Defender of the Year and was also named to the MLS Best XI team four times during his career. He also earned 28 caps with the United States Men's National Team and represented the USA at the 2006 FIFA World Cup.

"When I got traded to Kansas City in 2003, it was pretty shocking because I had been told there were big plans for me in San Jose. I didn't know where I was going to fit in KC. Preki won the MVP the year I got here, and we played in a 3-5-2 formation that was built around him and his skills. I know this sounds weird to say, but Preki breaking his leg was probably the best thing that ever happened to my career. With Preki out, we switched to a back four and I got to play my best position, and my career just took off from there. Had we stuck with the 3-5-2 formation, I just don't know if my trajectory would have been the same.

One of my favorite things about playing at Arrowhead Stadium was how well they kept the grass. It was immaculate. I have traveled around the world and played on some of the best surfaces in some of the biggest stadiums, and before the Chiefs got on the field in the late summer, that grass was as good as any field in the world. What's funny is that once the Chiefs started playing and there were these big 300-pound men out there, the field started to get run down, and the Chiefs had the audacity to blame us for the field conditions!

The Zardmeister was definitely the most bizarre thing I saw when we played at Arrowhead. My understanding is that the Zardmeister was Lamar Hunt's idea to get the fans going by having someone take the microphone and lead chants over the stadium's speakers. I think Lamar was ahead of his time, because those people are now known as capos, but the Zardmeister's chants were really bad. We would be playing and all of a sudden, the Zardmeister would chant things like, "Try, try, try to break the tie!" As players we didn't know what was happening. We thought, "What are we even hearing right now? Did someone steal the microphone at Arrowhead and is trying to make a mockery of everything?" I think that they used him for two games, and the fans were so upset that the Zardmeister disappeared, but he did not disappear from our memories.

Almost as memorable was the sponsorship activation we had during home games called the "Papa John's Magic Minutes." If someone on the Wizards scored between like minute 70 and minute 73—it was so exact—everybody at the stadium would get free pizza. It was such a short window of time to score, it was just ridiculous. But one game Stephen Armstrong scored during the Papa John's Magic Minutes, and I've never seen Arrowhead like that. Everybody was so fired up! And as players we knew right away that he had scored in the Magic Minutes. We wanted to find all the extra ticket stubs because we were going to raid Papa John's! I can't even explain how excited everybody was – it was pandemonium.

One of my biggest regrets is not being able to see the stadium project through. It would have been awesome to be a part of the name change to Sporting KC, and I would have been incredibly grateful to have walked out and been the first captain at the new stadium. Even though I didn't get that dream ending in KC, I was there in 2013 when we won MLS Cup. I had a field pass, and when we won, I jumped over the field boards and I was hugging everybody like I was a part of it. Any bitterness I had about how things ended, I just let it go and enjoyed that moment. I was so excited for the club, the fans and the ownership group, and I am so proud to still be a part of the club and to have been named a Sporting Legend.

COMMUNITYAMERICA BALLPARK
2008-2010

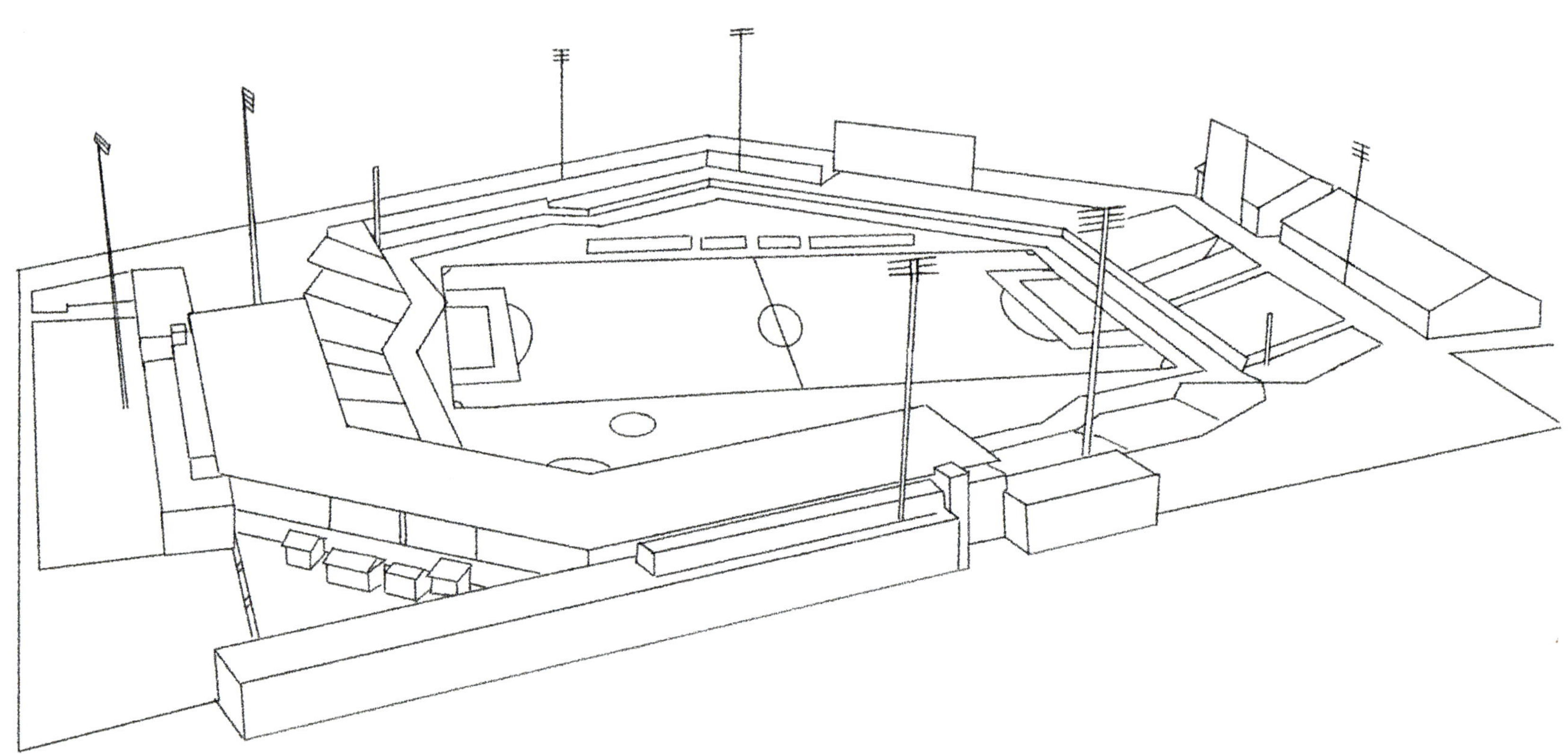

10,385
STADIUM CAPACITY

9,984
AVERAGE ATTENDANCE

19-13-12
RECORD [W-L-T]

"I actually really liked the intimacy of CommunityAmerica Ballpark compared to Arrowhead. The fans were your friends—you were so close to them. I remember having conversations during warmups each game with the same people in the VIP seats next to the coaching staff. We were able to have real and meaningful interactions with the fans in the Cauldron. I also scored a bunch of goals at CommunityAmerica Ballpark, so it's the best stadium I've ever played in!"

—JIMMY CONRAD

1993-2010

WIZARDS

A KANSAS CITY SOCCER TIMELINE

10.25.97
Preki named MLS MVP

09.05.98
Preki contributes to five goals with three goals and two assists

04.15.99
Ron Newman resigns; Ken Fogarty named interim manager

04.28.99
Bob Gansler named secnd head coach in Wizards history

05.15.99
Lamar Hunt awarded second-ever U.S. Soccer National Hall of Fame Medal of Honor

06.20.99
Chris Henderson records four assists in one match

12.17.93
Formation of Major League Soccer

06.06.95
Kansas City introduced as MLS charter member

10.17.95
MLS team names, logos, colors and uniforms unveiled in NYC

07.18.96
Wiz players don wigs in honor of "Carlos Valderrama Day" vs. the Tampa Bay Mutiny

Kansas City gets soccer franchise

SUMMER 94
FIFA World Cup 1994 in United States

10.11.95
Ron Newman named first head coach in MLS history

04.13.96
First match in Wiz history: 3 -0 win at Arrowhead vs. Colorado Rapids

11.18.96
Wiz officially become the Wizards

PRESEASON '00
Wizards trade for Jeff Baicher; He retires rather than reporting to Kansas City

09.06.00
Tony Meola earns 16th clean sheet of season in 1-0 W at NE – All-time MLS record

10.11.00
Bob Gansler named MLS Coach of the Year

10.15.02
Chris Klein named MLS Comeback Player of the Year

05.27.00
Tony Meola shutout streak reaches 681 minutes

09.09.00
Wizards secure Supporters Shield with 2-2 draw at Tampa Bay

10.10.00
Tony Meola named MLS MVP, Goalkeeper of the Year and Comeback Player of the Year; Peter Vermes named Defender of the Year

10.15.00
Wizards win MLS Cup 1-0 over the Chicago Fire at RFK Stadium

04.12.2003
The "Zardmeister" makes his debut

10.20.03
The "Zardmeister" quietly retired

11.21.03
Preki wins second MLS MVP award

09.22.04
Wizards win first U.S. Open Cup – 1-0 win at Arrowhead Stadium vs. Chicago

11.14.04
Wizards second MLS Cup appearance – 2-3 loss at Home Depot Center vs. D.C. United

12.09.04
Lamar Hunt announces team is for sale

12.12.04
Heart of America Soccer Foundation founded to "Save The Wizards"

03.02.07
Groundbreaking at Swope Park Training Facility

SPRING '07
Club launches KC Wizards Juniors Youth Development Program, which would later become the Sporting KC Academy

06.02.07
Eddie Johnson becomes first player in MLS History to score hat tricks in back-to-back games

11.05.07
Eddie Johnson named MLS Comeback Player of the Year

03.29.08
First game at CommunityAmerica Ballpark is 2-0 win vs. D.C. United

06.28.08
"Wizards of Waverly Place" star Selena Gomez makes special guest appearance at Wizards vs. Real Salt Lake

08.04.09
Curt Onalfo fired; Peter Vermes named interim manager

10.25.05
Jimmy Conrad named MLS Defender of the Year and Chris Klein named MLS Comeback Player of the Year

11.11.05
Tony Meola and Preki named to MLS All-Time Best XI as part of league's 10th anniversary

07.19.06
Bob Gansler resigns; Brian Bliss named interim manager

08.31.06
OnGoal, LLC purchases Wizards from Hunt Sports Group

11.27.06
Curt Onalfo named third head coach in Wizards history

12.13.06
Lamar Hunt dies at age 74 after long battle with cancer

09.09.09
Soccer-specific stadium plan unveiled for Kansas City, Kansas

11.06.09
Jimmy Conrad named MLS Humanitarian of the Year

11.09.09
Peter Vermes named fourth head coach in Wizards history

01.20.10
Groundbreaking at KC Soccer Stadium

Sports Daily

MAN WHO?

Herzog gets Hall welcome

New York reviews are mixed

BIG 12 FOOTBALL USHERS IN ERA OF CHANGE

07.25.10
Wizards defeat Manchester United 2-1

08.10.10
Preki inducted into U.S. Soccer National Hall of Fame

08.31.10
Wizards sign Jon Kempin as first Home Grown Player

11.17.10
Wizards name and logo removed from club website

WIZARDS KIT HISTORY
1996 - 2010

Nothing in sports is more representative of a team's identity than the uniform worn on a soccer pitch. Jerseys and designs become iconic and in many ways synonymous with the team wearing it and the city or country they represent.

The over-the-top aesthetics of the mid-'90s saw the Wiz/Wizards dressed in the now-classic and retro-cool rainbow motif, before giving way to the more refined Carolina Blue and white of the Bob Gansler-era, and eventually cobalt blue, dark indigo and yellow piping of the early OnGoal years.

adidas
WIZARDS
KANSAS CITY
2000-02
2002-03
2003-04
2004-05
2005
2006-07
2006-07
2008-09
2008-09
2010
2010

2006 - 2011

THE R

BIRTH

The Wizards had been saved in Kansas City, but the work was only just beginning. A decade after its inception, the team was still floundering, unable to gain much traction, even in a sports-mad city. But what some saw as an empty ledger, others viewed as a blank canvas. A new ownership group had a bold vision: Make Kansas City the premier club in Major League Soccer. The coming years would be focused on finding a new identity for the club and a new place in the Kansas City area to call home.

STARTING OVER

THE SEARCH FOR A NEW IDENTITY

The new owners had been in charge for less than six hours. The sale of the Club wouldn't be announced to the public until the following day, yet they were already facing a multimillion-dollar decision.

Lamar Hunt invited the families of the OnGoal group to join him in his owner's suite at Arrowhead Stadium for the Wizards vs. Red Bulls match the night of Aug. 30, 2006. It was part celebratory reception after signing the paperwork, part passing of the torch. In effect, Hunt's last match as the owner of the Wizards, and OnGoal's first. (The sale would be announced the next day.)

The mood was jubilant, and the champagne had been flowing. But then Clark Hunt spoke up.

"Hey, I need you to get on a conference call right now with me and (Deputy Commissioner of MLS) Ivan Gazidis," said Hunt. "Real Sociedad wants to buy Eddie Johnson. We've got an offer that you guys have to take a look at."

Johnson was a rising star in American soccer. He had made his MLS debut at only 17 years old and spent three seasons growing for FC Dallas before exploding with 12 goals at age 20 in 2004. He had also starred for the U.S. National Team in World Cup Qualifying, netting seven goals in his first six qualifiers. The Wizards acquired him in a trade prior to the 2006 season and while injuries and time away at the World Cup had limited his impact for Kansas City thus far, there was no question of his potential.

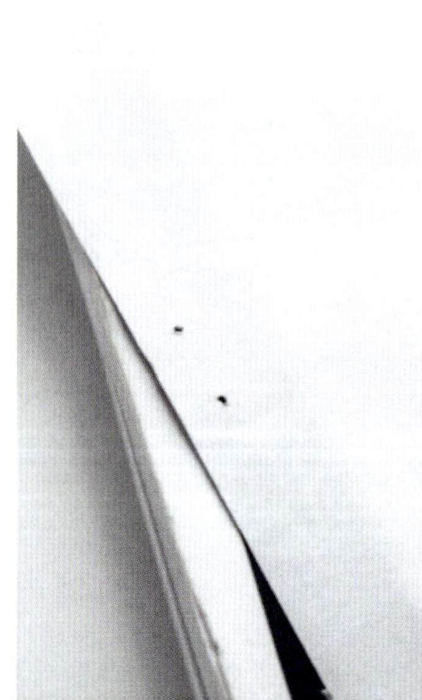

As the club's owners cast about for a new identity, the myriad of choices all eventually led back to the question, "What kind of club is this?"

Lamar Hunt, Neal Patterson and Cliff Illig at the ownership announcement in Overland Park, Kansas, Aug. 31, 2006.

it just opened up a Pandora's box of all this other uncertainty: Where we were playing, and where we were going to train, and who was going to be our coach, and what was the future going to look like? But it ended up paying off in a really meaningful way. I can't say enough about the ownership group and what they built and all the trials and tribulations to get there."

The Wizards struggled on the field throughout the 2006 season. Longtime coach Bob Gansler had been let go in the midst of a six-game losing streak in July, and assistant coach Brian Bliss took the helm on an interim basis for the rest of the year. The team performed admirably under Bliss, going 4-4-6 and fighting for a playoff spot until the end, but a loss on the final day of the season to the New York Red Bulls left them one point back and on the outside looking in.

The new ownership group had been relatively hands-off through the rest of the 2006 season, but the league was pressing them to name a president.

The OnGoal group huddled. They didn't have a soccer decision-maker yet. The future of one of American soccer's brightest young talents, and not insignificantly, their new club's most marketable asset, was up to a fresh group of owners less than a day into their tenure.

There really was only one possible answer, the group concluded. There was no way they could announce they were the new owners, and on the same day announce they were selling arguably the most talented player on the team. So they turned down Real Sociedad's offer.

The incident underscored the reality of the situation. This wasn't going to be easy.

"I don't think they exactly knew what they were walking into," said Wizards defender Jimmy Conrad. "Yes, it was great news … there was relief. But then

The standard structure in MLS since its inception had been similar to that of other U.S. sports leagues: A president and/or general manager who oversaw both the business and sports sides of the enterprise. In MLS, a recent trend had been to hire former American soccer icons after the relative success of Alexi Lalas in that role with the San Jose Earthquakes, New York Red Bulls and LA Galaxy.

Big names were discussed for the job, including high-profile former U.S. National Team players who made their interest public. They explored the options, interviewing several of those and a former GM of another MLS team the league had recommended, before ultimately deciding they felt better about charting their own path.

Peter Vermes would be the key.

Vermes, the former Wizards defender, had remained involved in the game in Kansas City. At the time, he was the Technical Director at Blue Valley Soccer Club in Overland Park. Throughout the two seasons the Wizards had been for sale, Vermes had even attended several Heart of America Soccer Foundation meetings and been around the "Save The Wizards" campaign.

Vermes and Robb Heineman first met as two people ostensibly interested in developing youth soccer fields in the Kansas City area, but Heineman kept turning the conversation to the professional side and posed a theoretical question.

"If you were running an MLS team," he asked Vermes, "how would the soccer side look?"

Vermes laid out his thoughts on a whiteboard at the front of the room. At the top of the chart it read "technical director," with a head coach below that and assistant coaches and levels of support staff on down the ladder.

"Back then, there was no such thing as the technical director as we know it," said Vermes. "So I put that all up on the board, and we kept going back and forth. We had a decent meeting. I left there thinking, 'if this guy is really going to build those fields, I think I want to be one of the guys to help run them.'"

Vermes' phone rang the next day. It was Heineman's assistant, inviting him back for another meeting the following afternoon. When he arrived, Heineman was sitting with a piece of paper face down on the table in front of him. As Vermes sat down, Heineman slid the paper across the table and turned it over. It was a professionally rendered version of the organizational structure they had sketched on the whiteboard earlier that week.

"Is this what you had in mind?" he asked.

"Yeah, it looks like that. But about those fields ..." responded Vermes, before Heineman cut in.

"What job do you want?"

"Excuse me?" asked Vermes, taken aback.

"We're buying the Wizards. What job do you want? Which one of these boxes do you see yourself in?" Heineman asked again, pointing at the paper. He was serious, and Vermes was a little stunned, but he knew what he had always wanted to do.

He pointed to the head coach box. "I'd want to be that guy."

"You can't be that guy," replied Heineman. "We don't want you to be that guy, because we might have to fire that guy, and you're too important to Kansas City from a soccer community perspective."

"Okay, then" said Vermes. "I'll be that guy."

Within a week of meeting the full ownership group, Vermes had signed on as a consultant, and on Nov. 15, 2006, he was named Technical Director of the Kansas City Wizards, a role he would come to redefine in MLS en route to earning the league's first-ever Sporting Executive of the Year award.

Johnson County residents rejected a 2006 bond propsal to develop a stadium and fields complex, which would have housed the Wizards. Opposition primarily focused on the amount of traffic it would bring.

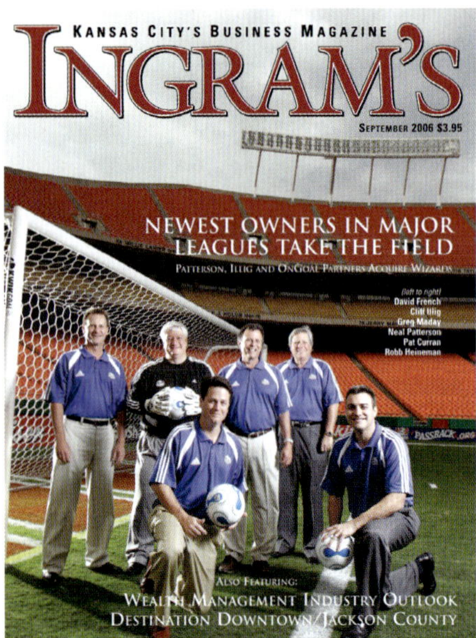

LESSONS LEARNED

In many ways, the decision to structure the organization this way would become a road map for the club: Listen to the advice of those around the league and American soccer who had been there before, but trust your own instincts. And, perhaps most importantly, learn from the history—and in many cases, mistakes—made by MLS and its clubs throughout its first 10 years.

While all involved knew a stadium was the ultimate target, the first step to changing the club was changing the perception around it both in the league and in the city. For the better part of eight years, people had been questioning the viability of the club and of Kansas City as a soccer market. The new ownership group and its new technical director knew they had to change the conversation from one of survival to one of aspiration. In his introductory press conference, Vermes aimed high.

"Our primary objective is to make this not only the model franchise in Major League Soccer, but also in the United States. Anyone who does not believe this can be done probably would not fit into the equation. Is this a one-year, three-year or five-year plan? We don't know yet, but I can tell you that we will be moving forward every minute we are on the field, working out or meeting."

The plan to make one of the league's lower-tier clubs into a paragon of the sport in the country was audacious, and it involved a three-prong approach: 1) Team; 2) Stadium; 3) Community.

The first step, if not the easiest, was to elevate the team side—the on-field product—to the next level. Leaning on wisdom gleaned from his time as a player both around the world and in MLS, Vermes was adamant the most immediate need was a new, dedicated training center.

For the previous few years, the Wizards had been splitting time sharing the Chiefs practice facility at Arrowhead and the public soccer field at telecom giant Sprint's world headquarters campus in Overland Park. It wasn't uncommon for the Wizards to wrap up training and immediately be replaced on the field by a lunchtime pick-up game of white-collar workers.

"If you want the players to be professionals, you have to make them feel like professionals," said Vermes. "You need someplace to call your home."

Home would be a new training center at Swope Park in Kansas City, Missouri. Announced in January 2007, as part of a partnership with the city Parks and Recreation Department, the Wizards built two dedicated fields for the professional team and renovated two more for public use. A 7,000-square-foot facility housed the locker room, coaching offices, training room, player lounge and a gym. Coincidentally, the land used had been the original front office and training center of the Chiefs when they moved to Kansas City in 1963, and the Wizards training home from 1998-2000.

"Those early years, we were really just trying to pull things together. Everybody was new," said

Vermes. Vermes was a first-year technical director, recently named Head Coach Curt Onalfo had never run a team of his own, and all three assistant coaches (including former Wizard Chris Henderson) were in their first job at the professional level. "So it was very chaotic. And oh my gosh, the hours … but getting that training facility done first and foremost was the key to everything."

On the stadium front, discussions were taking place with officials in both Johnson County, Kansas, and city leaders in Kansas City, Missouri, but nothing was signed yet. Either way, long-term tenancy in 79,000-seat Arrowhead Stadium was not sustainable. The financials were terrible, and even more importantly, so was the fan experience and atmosphere. Initially, OnGoal announced to season ticket holders a plan to construct a temporary stadium for the 2007 season, their first in charge of the club. The smaller, more intimate venue would help the Wizards to begin creating an environment and experience all their own, out from the shadow of the Chiefs in Arrowhead. It was a lesson the new owners had taken to heart from their discussions with Lamar Hunt.

The plan was to play in the temporary venue for a year or two while their new permanent stadium plans were finalized, and it was being built. But that plan changed before the season, and "home" for the 2007 season ended up Arrowhead once again, this time without the sweetheart financial deal of being the little brother to the Chiefs in the Hunt portfolio.

Off the field, the new leadership of the Wizards knew major changes were necessary to raise the club's profile in Kansas City, where the team was still a distant afterthought behind the Chiefs and Royals. More than a decade into the club's existence, its identity was still a problem; at least one owner had been known to call the Wizards soccer-ball-and-rainbow logo "the worst logo in professional sports" prior to the purchase of the team.

From as early as 2005, the then-prospective ownership group had agreed a rebrand would be necessary at some point. Ultimately, though, the change needed to be more than just the team's appearance. Many involved believed the Wizards brand had failed to grab hold because it lacked a compelling story.

The ownership group fully recognized the limitations around the Wizards name and visual identity. Coming in as relative outsiders allowed them a perspective those few in the weeds of soccer fandom in the city may not have had. They wanted to make it their own. And something in line with the vision they had for the club on a broader basis.

In many ways, the reasoning was similar to improving the on-field product and the stadium situation. The historic impression of the Wizards was one of unintentionally silly monikers and a rainbow motif and color palette that limited the ability to both sell merchandise and be taken seriously. The identity needed to change, and everyone knew that

Opposite, top: Illig, Maday, Jeanne Patterson and Heineman represented OnGoal alongside city officials at the Swope Park Training Center groundbreaking. Opposite, bottom: The ownership group was front-page business news in Kansas City. Below: Seating plans for a temporary stadium were developed and released to season ticket holders before the club opted to play the 2007 at Arrowhead.

process had to be taken with care and deliberation.

First crack at developing the new look was given to an agency out of New York City the league had engaged and had success with in the past. Beginning in December 2006, a small team inside the Wizards' offices held weekly calls with the branding firm. Vermes and ownership would join regularly.

Much of the focus of the discussions centered around developing a compelling identity that Kansas Citians could connect to. What made Kansas City special? The story came together around the city's unique location and history: two cities in two different states, brought together by common civic pride.

Within the city, if you asked a native Kansas Citian where they were from, you were likely to hear any of a myriad of neighborhoods or suburbs in response. But outside the city, ask a traveling Kansas Citian where they came from, and the answer was always the same: "Kansas City." Not Overland Park. Not Lee's Summit. In that situation, there was no Kansas City, Kansas, or Kansas City, Missouri. There was only "Kansas City." Importantly, this was true of the area's sports franchises as well.

This was the idea the group coalesced around and tried to drive home to the NYC branding firm. The concepts they received were not what they'd hoped for. The designs didn't feel relevant or authentic to Kansas City, or to the vision they had in their head for what the club could be.

Indeed, the very first set of logo concepts presented focused on the idea of the two states coming together, as requested. But the imagery and iconography was confusing. As they flipped through the presentation, one page in particular was hard to ignore: Across the top row of illustrations on page 16, a section titled "The City Unites," were bees. And not just bees, but bees with soccer ball thoraxes.

The design firm thought they had stumbled upon an idea. The honey bee was the Official State Insect of both Kansas and Missouri, the firm told them. And the shape of a bee's honeycombs were hexagons, just like the panels on a soccer ball. (Further confusing the issue, the logo concepts still said "Kansas City Wizards.")

Someone reached across the table and muted the conference call. The room full of longtime, and in some cases life-long, Kansas Citians asked one another if they had known the state insect of both states was the honeybee. It was unanimous; no one had had any idea. This was clearly not the direction.

Another set of proposed logo designs featured a bison and a mule, rearing up on their hind legs in a heraldic-looking pose. The bison and the mule were the state animals of Kansas and Missouri, respectively, explained the firm. By the end of the day, others in the office had heard about the bee and bison/mule drawings and were begging to see the logos. The name "Kansas City Ticklish Bison" became somewhat of a running joke throughout the early days.

Page 16 of the initial branding presentation focused on the concept of "The City Unites" and featured the state insects and animals of Kansas and Missouri.

Over the course of the next several months, another five rounds of logo concepts were explored with the firm from New York, some in color, some in black-and-white, all missing the mark in some fashion. Ownership was beginning to feel strongly that the character of the brand had to be something different than the traditional American sports mascot. And nothing the branding firm had presented was particularly likely to resonate more than the current Wizards concept. By March the firm was off the job, and the project was back to square one, with more lessons learned.

Eschewing the symbolism of a mascot and not wanting to create just another interlocking "KC," the group knew it would need to find a unique way to represent Kansas City in the new mark. From the beginning, they had been drawn to a graphical representation of the state line that separates the states of Kansas and Missouri. For nearly 200 years, this invisible dividing line created by the confluence of two major rivers had shaped the city's story. Lewis and Clark had camped at its junction, the starting point of their expedition to the great American western frontier. Blood had been spilled and wars had been fought over it. It was uniquely Kansas City. No other city in the world could claim ownership. And by building a mark centered around the incredible history of the shared border where these two states and cities came together, it could be a unifying point. Two states, one city. United by the divide.

Scribbling on a napkin at an after-work happy hour, they had stumbled across something they felt had meaning. A diagonal line angled down to the right represented the winding Missouri River at the northern section of the border, before breaking sharply downward at the point where the Missouri meets the Kansas River. It was stylized, it was unique, and once you saw it, you couldn't help but be drawn to how it represented Kansas City.

In an effort to sell more merchandise, a new cobalt blue and dark indigo with yellow trim color palette was developed by adidas and would be rolled out for the 2008 season.

They had pitched it to the New York City branding firm, who had explored it in a few concepts and logo iterations, but clearly didn't feel the same investment. With the New York firm out of the picture, the "state line" element became the focus of the Wizards' front office visual identity discussions, but it would take another three years before it would be fully realized. With stadium plans in discussion, the decision was made to focus on getting the stadium approved first so they could launch a new brand in conjunction with a new stadium.

While these early conversations about a new identity were taking place, equipment and jersey supplier adidas came to the team with a suggestion to change the club's present shade of blue. The Wizards had been wearing a bright blue since the 2000 season when they began the transition away from the rainbow motif. But adidas only carried it in certain fabrics, meaning it wasn't available for all of the club's needs, like training tops and sideline apparel. Changing to a darker shade would allow for more consistency and open up the option to carry

Plans for the Wizards stadium at Three Trails/Bannister Mall included a plaza that opened directly into the stadium and an old-English style pub, bottom right.

more merchandise for fans in the same hue.

Merchandise was certainly an area with potential for growth. The Wizards' shade of blue was distinctive in MLS, but nothing was selling. In 2006 the club placed the minimum order of 72 jerseys from adidas to sell in the team store. Over the course of the season, even that small supply hadn't sold out.

Adidas suggested a deeper, cobalt blue to replace the brighter shade. And they introduced a new dark indigo secondary color and bright yellow accent trim for jerseys and on-field equipment. The club agreed, and the process was put in motion for the 2008 season. At the same time, the team began to phase out the rainbow-ball logo in favor of a simpler shield with "Kansas City" stacked over the existing "Wizards" in the custom club typeface.

The 2007 season felt, in large part, not very different from the years before it in Arrowhead. The first-day decision by OnGoal to not sell star Eddie Johnson turned out to be prescient, and he delivered to the tune of 15 goals, including back-to-back hat tricks in weeks eight and nine. The team made the playoffs and advanced past Chivas USA in the first round before falling to eventual champion Houston 2-0 in the Conference Finals. But throughout the season, the struggle to put fans in the building continued. By the end of the year, the Wizards had finished dead last in attendance once again, more than 2,500 fans per game behind their closest competitor.

New ownership group, exciting team, return to playoff soccer, same problems in the stands.

THE STOPGAP

The off-field future of the Wizards started to look more promising in the middle of the 2007 season with the club's announcement of a plan to develop a stadium, fields and retail complex at the site of the old Bannister Mall in southeast Kansas City, Missouri. The complex would be financed by a combination of public and private funds, with a financing tool designed to bring development to blighted areas. It seemed a win-win for the city and the soccer team—the reclamation of a once vibrant, now dormant, corridor of town and a permanent home of their own for the club. Development on the project, valued at nearly $950 million, was set to begin as soon as the bonds were backed to fund it.

With the new training center open and a stadium seemingly imminent, it was time to finally move out of Arrowhead and begin building a new fan experience for the future. The new stadium would house 18,000-20,000 fans, so the search for a more intimate temporary venue in Kansas City began in earnest. The answer came in the most unlikely of places: a baseball stadium in Kansas City, Kansas.

CommunityAmerica Ballpark was home to the Kansas City T-Bones, a minor league team in the unaffiliated Northern League. The stadium was one piece of the Legends Shopping District, part of the economic development spurred on by the 2001 opening of Kansas Speedway, which had turned western Wyandotte County from farmland into a retail and tourism destination.

"CAB" was small, seating only 6,500 for baseball. But it was in a vibrant, family-friendly location just down the highway from soccer-mad Johnson County, and it had the ability to be renovated to hold a larger crowd. Given that the Wizards had averaged just over 10,000 fans the year before at Arrowhead, "slightly larger" would suit nicely.

With the addition of a large bleacher over the left field (baseball) wall, field-side seating for a "premium" experience next to the pitch and sod to cover the necessary sections of the baseball diamond, the Wizards were able to convert it into a 10,385-seat venue for soccer. Perfect for the fanbase at the time.

The conversion itself, however, was daunting, taking 24 to 72 hours in total, depending on the circumstances. And it had to be done for every single match. If the Wizards were scheduled to play Saturday evening at 7:30, and the T-Bones played Thursday night, as was often the case, the move-in for stadium conversion would begin within minutes of the final out of the baseball game. An army of Wizards staffers, interns and part-time workers would descend on the ballpark, working throughout the days and into the nights, to convert a maroon-themed baseball stadium into a blue soccer stadium, complete with a large vinyl replica of a Wizards jersey over home plate and a 35-foot-tall banner covering up the center field "batter's eye."

On the pitch, the soccer itself was sometimes hard to take seriously—not due to the quality on the field (though that lagged at times because of the awkwardly small field squeezed in between the pitcher's mound and outfield warning track)—but because of all the other distractions. Past the right field wall was a playground, complete with monkey bars, rings and slide. In left field, not 20 yards from the sideline, were two portable toilets, ostensibly for the "premium seating" field-side guests. They also happened to be the facilities closest to the player benches. In his rookie year of 2009, a young Matt Besler was once spotted waiting, in full kit and cleats, for the current occupant of the men's room to vacate. He would check into the match minutes later.

"Sometimes you have to take a step backwards to go forward," said Kerry Zavagnin, a player on the 2008 team and an assistant coach in 2009. "I understood that it was a temporary solution to what was hopefully a permanent solution down the road. But that was tough. CAB was really tough."

For the 2008 season, the oversized banner featured the smiling face of the Wizards' new headline player, Argentinean star Claudio Lopez, who had been signed as the club's first "designated player."

Owner Cliff Illig and then-Technical Director Peter Vermes before a match at CommunityAmerica Ballpark.

Fans in the Cauldron at CommunityAmerica Ballpark were just yards away from the goal line, prompting moments like this one where goalscorer Ivan Trujillo leapt into the stands to celebrate his first Wizards goal.

Better known as "the Beckham Rule," the designated player mechanism allowed MLS teams to sign big-name players and only apply a small portion of their pay to the salary cap. Lopez had starred in Italy, Spain and his native Argentina, not to mention alongside the likes of Ronaldo, Ronaldinho and Thierry Henry in the famous "Secret Tournament" Nike soccer global ad campaign. He was arguably the highest-profile player to yet don a Wizards uniform.

But he would not be the biggest star to wear a Wizards jersey in CommunityAmerica Ballpark that year. The club's marketing had begun to evolve. Still focusing on a family audience, the team had started looking to splashier promotions. The highlight for many of the under-15 set in 2008 was undoubtedly the visit of Disney Channel's Selena Gomez. A decade before she would be named Billboard's Woman of the Year, Gomez put on the new cobalt blue Wizards jersey and drew thousands to a meet-and-greet at the June 28 match against Real Salt Lake. The capacity crowd was only the third official "sell out" in Wizards history.

"She was on the cusp of being a star, but you could already tell she was going to be even bigger," said Jimmy Conrad. "And just for her to be there with her family, signing in a little booth is super funny to me."

The Wizards made the playoffs, but it never felt like a team capable of contending for silverware, and they were knocked out in the first round by the Supporters Shield and eventual-MLS Cup winning Columbus Crew.

Things didn't improve the next season. Onalfo was dismissed as the head coach during August in the midst of a four-match winless streak and following a 6-0 loss to Dallas, and Vermes took over the duties as interim head coach. But the die was cast, and the Wizards missed the playoffs. In the stands, however, things were starting to feel different.

"Yes, it didn't feel professional in a lot of different ways," said Conrad. "But it did feel like 'something's changing here in Kansas City.' We're not there yet. But we were all in that together, man. We were all trying to push the sport forward by making something happen there."

The fanbase was evolving. The Cauldron, due to the awkward dimensions of the stadium layout, were just feet away from the back of the net. It had more than doubled in size since the move from Arrowhead and was getting more organized. And rowdy.

The fans and players were, perhaps, starting to feel like they were a part of something together. A true supporters culture was on the verge of forming.

"There was no 'church and state,'" said Conrad. "It was cozy. It was nice to go jump into the stands. You know, I was the first person to do that. After I scored I did a little bit of the 'Lambeau Leap' into the Cauldron, which was very cool. And then you have these special moments like when David Beckham played there one time and it was pandemonium."

It's true. The biggest soccer icon on the planet once played a game in front of a bursting-at-the-seams crowd of 11,906 fans at a minor league baseball stadium. The match was entertaining to boot. The Wizards and LA Galaxy thrilled spectators in a 1-1 draw in which Beckham assisted U.S. legend Landon Donovan, and Lopez scored for the Wizards from beyond midfield.

But the most pressing concerns were coming off the field, as the once-promising stadium plans at the Bannister location began to look bleak. The financial collapse of 2008 had decimated the retail market. Without anchor retail tenants to help generate revenue at the complex, there was little outside interest in financing the bonds to pay for the project. Wizards Ownership and its representatives were at City Hall almost daily working to recut the deal, but nothing came to fruition. The Wizards' Bannister Mall stadium project was dead.

But as the 2009 season was kicking off, a new opportunity arose. Down the road from CAB was the Kansas City branch of Nebraska Furniture Mart, the Warren Buffet-owned retail giant. NFM owned a plot of land across the street from their existing parking lots on which they had always planned to build overflow parking or work with the right retail development. With the Wizards' Bannister stadium plan dead, and the land sitting empty, NFM saw an opportunity. A soccer stadium bringing hundreds of thousands of visitors annually to the area, meant hundreds of thousands of potential customers coming into their backyard.

NFM wanted to give the Wizards the land. And because it was within the boundaries of the bond district used to build up the area, there was existing sales tax revenue that allowed them to sell the bonds to construct the stadium.

It was a small plot of land, not large enough for the stadium and fields complex combination they had planned. "Can you really fit a stadium on this postage stamp?" Wizards owner Neal Patterson asked when he first viewed the site. But the stadium had always been the key. All the way back to Lamar Hunt's early conversations with the ownership group and especially his dinner with Patterson and Illig in '06, he had stressed the need for a dedicated venue and the fan experience opportunities that came along with it. Nothing was more important than "a committed environment," as Hunt described it.

As the summer of 2009 went on, the plans for the Kansas City, Kansas stadium option fell into place. In a Sept. 9 post on the Wizards website, the team announced it had agreed to a deal to build an ultra-modern soccer-specific stadium at the location offered by Nebraska Furniture Mart. The stadium was planned to open sometime in the summer of 2011, they said, and ownership sought input from fans about the kind of experiences they wanted in Kansas City's new soccer cathedral.

It was an aggressive timeline. Stadiums of the size and scope envisioned typically took 22 to 24 months to be built. The Wizards were planning to do it in only 18. By mid-December, bulldozers were on site in preparation for construction, which began in February 2010. By that spring, steel was being raised at what was clearly the most ambitious soccer-specific stadium the country had ever seen, a $200-million love letter to the game and its fans.

Disney Channel star Selena Gomez's visit brought a sellout crowd to CommunityAmerica Ballpark.while the 35-foot-tall banner of Claudio Lopez looked on.

STADIUM DESIGN

As the stadium continued to take shape, the Club worked closely with its fanbase, asking for input and creating the types of amenities and experiences they were looking for. Designing the stadium for "people" and "experiences" was paramount.

The stadium road map all started with defining the vision—Illig's vivid description of a future state: "The first world-class soccer stadium in the United States."

The overriding theme in the stadium development was to push the definition of what soccer could be in America—to take it to the next level. The goal was to combine the best pieces of the European soccer model—a dramatic roof canopy that covers all seats, minimal seating in the corners to optimize fans' views of the pitch, a rounded locker room where no player will feel lesser or greater than another—but with a genuine American feel.

Early watercolor renderings show the player walkout through the Field Club much as it would come to be built. The Wizards' opponents in the paintings resemble Manchester United.

The stadium design coalesced around four principle philosophies:

- End-to-end design
- Sweat the details
- Push your people out front
- Sprinkle in a few "magic moments"

Ownership was also active on social media and the BigSoccer message boards, requesting insight from fans about what they wanted to see in the new stadium and from their soccer club.

The stadium development team created dozens of "programs" around the different types of fans who would attend games, and the goal became designing that fan experience from the moment they got out of their car to go in to the moment they exited the stadium after the match. Eventually, they presented ownership, particularly Illig and Patterson who had great admiration for the "Disney Model" and were specially focused on fan experience, with a workbook full of these proposed programs, and it became the bible throughout the stadium's development.

One of its bigger sections was on the idea of a supporters bar: A "Members Club" for the diehard fans—the Cauldron—to have a space of their own. A sports bar with lots of TVs and cheaper beer and food as a reward for helping create the stadium matchday atmosphere.

Another program was designed around the most premium ticketed area, a "Field Club" with all-inclusive food and beverages. Field Club seats would be at the level of the playing surface and immediately next to the benches. The player pre-match processional would walk straight through the heart of the indoor Field Club space. It's a concept that would make its debut at Jerry Jones Cowboys Stadium in 2010, and arguments persist whether Jones "adopted" it from conversations with Patterson and Illig, or the other way around.

"Every design decision we made was directed back toward the fan experience," said Jon Knight, senior principal at architecture firm Populous, and one of the stadium's chief designers. "It was by paying special attention to even the littlest details that got us to this result—it's not just a stadium; it's a social experience."

Aesthetically, the stadium was designed to capture the movement and motion of the beautiful game. "The body and the ball."

Based on the concept of stop-motion photography, the angular aluminum fins on the exterior represent the players' body and athleticism, while the iconic rising roof canopy is designed to invoke the feeling of a ball in flight.

Nearly everything about the stadium was modeled in 3-D to make sure it fit perfectly and would not interrupt the carefully planned aesthetics or the fan experience.

Every detail, down to the placement and design of speakers and light fixtures in the seating bowl, was planned to be as integrated as possible, with no "hanging" parts. Fixtures in the front of the roof canopy were painted light sporting blue to not distract the eye, while speakers mounted further back on the roof were colored dark blue to match the trusses on which they were hung.

THE POWER OF "WE"

The new stadium plan finally secured, and the stadium fully under construction, it was time to renew focus on the rebrand. Work had never really stopped, of course. The intervening years had been spent further examining the big picture question of "what kind of franchise they wanted to be" going forward. All agreed if they were going to live up to their stated goal of being the model franchise in MLS and American soccer, they couldn't approach it the same way as everybody else.

"How do we get people to be a part of the brand, not a fan of the brand?" ownership would often ask.

A theme began to develop: The biggest sports entities in the world were all driven by dynamic fan bases with a clear sense of belonging and investment in everything the club does—on and off the field. They were part of something larger than themselves. More than fans, they were part of the club. The current fanbase called the team "the Wizards." The future meant creating a place where people felt a sense of ownership and belonging. Where people would say "We." The idea of creating a "modern sports club" in American soccer was born.

"The owners always had a vision of wanting to create this club that was very inclusive," said Andy

The stadium's rising roofline is designed to resemble the floating arc of a ball in flight, while the metal fins on the exterior represent the body of a player.

"Phase 01" from adidas' brand team in September '09, presented the team with a purple color concept.

Tretiak, the club's vice president of marketing from 2010-2016. "It wasn't exclusive in that it was only going to be for a certain group of people who were hugely passionate about soccer. They wanted to make an organization that everybody would feel a part of in some way. Not only coming to games and cheering for the team, but also helping build it from the ground up."

They had been zeroing in on the idea of calling the team "Kansas City Soccer Club," until Heineman pitched the group on the idea of Sporting Club instead. When a marketing consultant suggested they do market research and focus group the name, they rejected the idea out of hand, expecting they already knew what the research would tell them: Many initial reactions would be that they were trying to rip off a European-style name. But they felt strongly that if they built things the right way, they could succeed. If the team was good on the field, the stadium was beautiful, and they embedded themselves in the community, they could create something that was different and sustainable.

A new and more detailed concept of the Sporting Club idea began to take shape. "Season Ticket Holders" would be called "Members" in the Club, and those members would be engaged in unique ways and provided benefits.

By late summer 2009, things were proceeding again on the visual identity front as well. Adidas had recently launched an internal department dedicated to identity and branding, and the club had begun engaging with this group. With nearly two years of internal discussions under their belt, they came to the conversations with adidas armed with a clearer picture of the aesthetic they were going for and a more complete vision and story. The new working partnership clicked very early on.

The look began to focus immediately around the use of an interlocking "SC" (for Sporting Club) inspired by the Spanish-influenced architecture of Kansas City's famous Country Club Plaza. The group spent a lot of time exploring the shape of the badge, looking at everything from completely unique asymmetrical shapes to standard circles and roundels. The "state line" motif stayed constant throughout, an important connection to the city.

A large part of the discussions in early fall 2009 were about color palettes. The Wizards had experience with, quite literally, every color under the rainbow and had gone through a seemingly ever-changing set of blues until the recent adoption of cobalt. Ownership, however, was interested in exploring new color concepts, due to the similarity between cobalt and the shades of blue associated with the Royals and Kansas Jayhawks. Something more uniquely identifiable was needed.

A single, full-day session in September was pivotal in the development of the new identity. Adidas had flown executives, product designers and their branding team to Kansas City to present concepts to Wizards brass and ownership. As they passed around the presentation booklets, eyebrows raised among the Kansas City team gathered in the room. The cover was a picture of the city skyline with the words “Sporting Club of Kansas City” across it. The whole thing was shaded purple.

It was “eggplant,” not purple, explained an adidas rep. Darker and more regal than traditional royal purple, and offset with gold and white, it would be a completely unique color palette in American soccer. It could tie into Kansas City’s “royal” heritage for sports teams and fit with the Spanish-architecture influenced look of the design elements.

After a nearly eight-hour session, during which logo design concepts were further developed and “state line” design elements were decided upon for the inaugural jerseys with the new name, a voice spoke up from a corner of the room. “Are we really going to be a purple soccer team?”

A small group, which included Michael Illig, had been at the back of the room ruminating on the color palette. A standing rule in the branding discussions, adopted from one of Patterson’s “Neal-isms,” was “propose, don’t oppose.” Knowing they couldn’t bring up a problem unless they were also able to present a workable solution, soon the group were making the case there was heritage in the club’s history around being a blue soccer team. They presented the larger group with an alternative: Stick with blue, but move to a light blue, similar to Argentina’s traditional color. It, too, was unique in American soccer at the time, and the club could have the ability to “own it” if they wanted. Pair it with the dark indigo shade the Wizards had been using recently as a secondary color and accent it with either a silver or gold to set things off. “The light blue/dark blue/gray would be a classic ‘Cary Grant suit’ color palette,” one of the Adidas apparel designers said, and that seemed to seal it as the direction the room wanted to go, even though gold remained on the table for a few more months.

The Adidas crew had work to do. They had come to town planning to walk away with marching orders to further explore logo concepts and jerseys for a purple soccer team and ended up with a classic light blue/dark blue club. Over the following weeks and months, there was a sprint to finalize the jerseys as they typically required an 18- to 24-month production timeline, and the Club was planning a launch in time for the 2011 season and the new stadium opening. The design would be clean and simple at launch, with a subtle, single needle-stitched “state line” on the collared light blue primary kit and an embossed pattern featuring the “SC” in a filigree on the dark blue secondary.

A variety of logo concepts were based on Kansas City’s Spanish-inspired architecture.

The "Phase 01 Recap" confirms the choice of the blue color palette and "SC" ligature elements.

The logo was taking longer to come together. A "state line" element and the "SC" were ever-present, but the wrapper surrounding them was debated for months. In early spring 2010, things were getting close, and the design group brought the logo work to Kansas City agency Barkley to help get it across the finish line.

The symbolism and the narrative were the primary focus. Extensive meetings were held to discuss every intricate detail. One two-plus-hour meeting focused exclusively on the number of stripes and the direction they were going.

The club had finally landed on a shape, modeled after the upside-down teardrop of the initial "Wiz" logo, and designers at Barkley helped refine the mark, cleaning up the "SC" interlock and the state line stripes and offering a more modern typeface. By summer they had a logo. Mostly. The intent all along had been for the club to be officially called Sporting Club Kansas City, casually shortened to "Sporting Kansas City" as is the norm with similarly named clubs around the world. But the league's lawyers had run into problems with trademarking the name. "Sporting Kansas City" was trademarkable. "Sporting Club" was not. Sporting Kansas City it would be.

A plan to announce the new identity following the 2010 season was developed. But in the meantime, the summer of 2010 had begun to give Kansas Citians a glimpse of what soccer fandom in their city could be. The first big indicator that the culture of the sport was changing came during that summer's World Cup when relatively small watch parties of several hundred for early-round U.S. matches hosted by the Wizards at the downtown Power & Light District ballooned as the Yanks advanced further in the tournament. By the knockout round match versus Ghana, the watch parties in KC had become the face of soccer fandom in America all over the world, and ESPN had dispatched reporter Pedro Gomez to the site as more than 12,000 turned the venue into a raucous party.

The other game-changer came in July, when the opportunity to face global soccer giant Manchester United presented itself. The Wizards jumped at the chance, and the team parlayed the news that the world's most popular team was coming to Kansas City into a massive ticket drive for the following season in the new stadium, selling more than 1,600 season tickets in a single day.

On July 25, in front of a Kansas City-record soccer crowd of 52,424 at Arrowhead, the Wizards shocked the soccer world with a 2-1 victory behind goals from Davy Arnaud and Kei Kamara. The true highlight of the day, though, was the shift in the crowd as the Wizards held on to the lead late. A stadium that had started the game with the sounds of Manchester United chants had suddenly flipped, and the KC natives, many of whom were wearing the red of the English giants, were joining along with the singing Wizards faithful in the Cauldron behind the goal. It would prove to be a seminal moment and set the table for what was to come.

A SECOND CHANCE AT A FIRST IMPRESSION

The night of the Wizards rebrand announcement, Nov. 17, 2010, was cold. But not as cold as the reception to the new name that the club was expecting from some factions of the Wizards fanbase.

"I was driving down there, and Cliff called me and said, 'I hope you're ready for this. Some of these fans are not going to be excited,'" recalls Heineman. "So, it's a name we knew some people would probably be pretty cool to at the start."

There had been cold feet from some in the front office and even the ownership up until the final days.

"How do you not have a mascot? How do you not have a 'Kansas City Somethings?' people asked," said Vermes. "I told them, 'Ah, we'll be fine.'"

As he sat backstage at the Living Room at Power & Light District, Heineman knew he was announcing more than just a new name and logo, he was launching a new idea. He was introducting a concept of membership and what it meant to be part of the club that was very different from what anybody else in American sports had been doing. Moreover, it was still very aspirational at that point.

The backdrop of the stage was a giant wall of soccer balls, 30 rows tall and 40 rows wide, that concealed the new logo from the crowd. The wall was rigged so that the exact moment the name was announed, the balls would all fall, revealing the new Sporting Kansas City mark. At least that was the plan. Given the secrecy of the logo leading up to the event (it had leaked online to a small portion of the Wizards fan crowd, but the vast majority of the city had not seen it or heard the new name), they had been unable to test the wall, so nobody was really sure what would happen when it was triggered.

"We'd be remiss if we didn't try to push the edge of the envelope with what we're trying to do with sports," Heineman said to the crowd of several thousand gathered that evening. "We believe a change in identity for the club is necessary to effectively live and breathe this vision."

"We are Missouri. We are Kansas. We're the people's game in Kansas City. You have our pledge that we'll do everything we can to be the finest in Major League Soccer. We are Sporting Kansas City."

And with that, the balls dropped, and the Sporting Kansas City era began to cheers (and a few scattered "boos"). The Sporting (née Wizards) Academy players immediately jumped on stage to help distribute the souvenir balls to the fans in attendance. They had been instructed to toss the balls to the waiting audience, but as kids are wont to do, they began to wing them into the the crowd as hard as they could. One wayward ball hit the MetroSports camera and

Dozens of variations on the state line pattern were considered, all including 11 lines either literally or figuratively.

broke it. The effect of of the ball distribution was beautiful, but the process may not have been as well thought out.

The jerseys were unveiled next, with newly signed Mexican star Designated Player Omar Bravo and long-time Wizards captain Jimmy Conrad as the models. (Ironically, Conrad would be traded before the 2011 season began, and never actually play a match in the jersey he helped debut.)

As the event went on, the news started making its way around the internet. While most who were at the event to hear the story around membership and the future of the Club left that evening feeling happy, the reactions from the rest of the city and country were not as positive.

Below: Soccer balls fly through the air after the wall shielding the logo falls. Opposite: The untested wall of 120 soccer balls worked to perfection, dropping in waterfall fashion to reveal the logo at the exact moment Heineman proclaimed, "We are Sporting Kansas City."

Deadspin described the rebrand as "impossibly awful." The most discussed reaction in Kansas City was that of longtime TV sportscaster Jack Harry. Harry had been given a sneak peek of the new identity earlier in the week and had told the club's staff he thought it was unique and different and had a "real chance to be successful." But when he opened his sports segment that evening, the graphic over his shoulder read "Sporting Wha?!" and he did not hold back with his criticisms of the club's new name, saying he just didn't understand what he was supposed to call the team. (It should be noted that within the year, Harry had aired a public mea culpa segment apologizing for his initial reaction given the club and stadium's success.)

But by that point, those on the inside—from the ownership group to Vermes to the players and support staff—had all bought into the transformation.

"I vividly remember where I was standing at the Power & Light District," said Matt Besler. "It was like the snap of a finger. All of a sudden we became a different team and organization."

All involved recognized the audacious endeavor they were taking part in and realized that some of the initial criticism was inevitable. They also recognized that they had the ace in the hole, the magnificent new stadium that would open in months.

Now with a new identity and a clear vision of what the Club was going to be, the table was set. It was up to them to live up to the promises they had made on the field, to the fans and in the community. Only then could the success of the rebrand truly be measured. ♦

KANSAS CITY
KANSAS CITY
SPORTING

adidas
RESPONSE
adidas
adidas

MY STORY: JIMMY NIELSEN

2012 U.S. Open Cup
2013 MLS Cup

A two-time MLS All-Star, Jimmy Nielsen was MLS Goalkeeper of the Year and a Best XI selection in 2012. The White Puma captained the club to championships in 2012 and 2013 and his 0.99 goals against average is the lowest in MLS history among goalkeepers with 15 games played.

"You can call it love at first sight. My time with Sporting was so much better than I ever could have expected.

When I joined Kansas City from Denmark in 2010, some people in my homeland said, "Well, you're going to a retirement league." I'll be honest, that was kind of how I viewed it too. But after my first conversation with Peter Vermes, he definitely changed my point of view. It was one of the most motivating phone calls I have ever had, and after a few hours of talking, we had a deal made for me to join the team.

I had no idea about Kansas City. When I was speaking to Peter on the phone, he had me pull out a map so I could find Kansas City. He said, "Do you know where New York is? Well, just move your finger towards the middle of the country. When you find the middle, there you go—Kansas City."

I linked up with the team in Arizona for preseason. We trained there for a few days and then returned to Kansas City. That's where I experienced CommunityAmerica Ball Park, our home baseball stadium, for the first time. And I'm like, "Oh, Jesus Christ." But it ended up not being that bad. It was a fun little environment.

Of course, the real game-changer was when we moved into Sporting Park. You just had that special feeling week after week when you got to the stadium. It was something you looked forward to like a little kid looked forward to Christmas. When you walked into that stadium, you felt like you were bulletproof. When it was rocking, it was the most intense stadium in the league. There may have been 60,000 people in Seattle's stadium, but I didn't feel the same intensity from the fans like I did here. They gave us that extra boost every night.

During my Sporting career, I don't remember one game where we hadn't given absolutely everything we had. We left it all on the field. That was always the identity of our team. We also had tremendous training habits and an excellent locker room atmosphere. We had a very good time with each other off the pitch, but at training and in games, we held each other accountable.

Kansas Citians take so much pride in their sports teams. They wear that pride under their skin. The Kansas City community is full of friendly, hardworking people who will support you for life. It was always easy for them to recognize the hard work we put in as a team. In that respect, we shared the same identity. Competing at Children's Mercy Park was something we did together. At Sporting, it's not just the team, the players and the organization. The whole city is behind us.

To this day, before I fall asleep every night, I can still feel the ground under my feet shaking from the game when we beat Seattle in the 2012 Lamar Hunt U.S. Open Cup Final. The noise just before Seattle's Eddie Johnson took his penalty is probably the loudest experience I've had at a stadium. The place was shaking like a little earthquake. Sometimes when I go to sleep, I feel that same shock in my body, and I relive that moment for a few seconds. And then I just turn over in bed with a little smile on my face and fall asleep.

Winning the MLS Cup and painting the wall in 2013 was a very proud moment, of course. In speaking with others about the game, I have heard the line, "I was there" so many times that you'd think 250,000 people were in the stadium that night. It was a very tough 120 minutes for me to get through because my ribs were hurting, and it was so ridiculously cold. It's not very often that I get emotional, but I got emotional that night because I celebrated with the feeling that this was my very last game.

My four years with Sporting were incredible on and off the field—some of the best times of my life. Everything about it was absolutely amazing.

SNAPSHOT
OPENING NIGHT
JUNE 9, 2011

1) Inaugural Match ticket in the Members' Stand for the opening night of Livestrong Sporting Park, June 9, 2011.

2) Kansas City icon Ida McBeth performed a stunning rendition of the national anthem.

3) Match ball from opening night, June 9, 2011.

4) Promotional poster advertising the match as well as a pre-match concert on the plaza by Kansas City alt-rock band The Republic Tigers

5) The team huddle before the first match in their new home.

6) Local artist Mike Savage's painting honored the occasion in a commemorative poster presented to all who attended.

7) Late in the match, there was a pitch invasion by a man dressed as a cow.

1

2

3

4

5

6

7

adidas
SPORTING
MLS
Ivy
INVESTMENTS

MY STORY: ROGER ESPINOZA

Getting drafted in 2008 was an unbelievable moment. In the back of my mind, my attitude was, "I'm not going to let the Wizards down. They took a chance on me, and I'm going to go there and give everything I got every single day." I was just grateful that they took an opportunity to take me.

I *did* know about Kansas City. In JUCO before you start a season, they do a tournament of the teams they expect to be highly ranked. At the time, Johnson County Community College was one of those teams. When we were in Kansas City, our coach took us to Jack Stack BBQ and to a Royals baseball game. And I vividly remember he also took us to the Negro Leagues Baseball Museum —a very amazing place. And when we were leaving town, I remember running into the Wizards players at the airport.

CommunityAmerica Ballpark is always going to be a place that I cherish just because that's where I got my opportunity. That's where fans were first yelling my name. There are so many stories about CAB: Playing on the baseball field, and the field not being the right size. It was so small that you could kick a ball across the field pretty easily. It felt like there were more than 11 players on each side. That's a good way to describe it. People celebrating goals like they had hit a home run. I hate to say it, Gerso, but you were not the first one.

Sporting had picked up Seth (Sinovic) right before I left for the [2011] Gold Cup, and he was a left back, so I kind of had an idea that when I got back I might not have my position, because Seth was killing it. And then I moved to the middle, and right away it felt like a position I belonged in.

After the bad loss in 2011 in the playoffs to Houston, everybody came mentally prepared to play in 2012. We'd had a good start to the season and then Peter came in one day before our first Open Cup game and told us we're going to go win the whole thing. "We are going to win this tournament. Every game in front of us, we are going to try to win. It doesn't matter if it's a preseason friendly, if it's a college team, doesn't matter. Every game we play, there's no friendlies in this world."

Before the final in 2012, I remember everybody in the locker room was ready to go to war. Every single player knew that we were not going to lose that game at home. Finals for us have been beyond special. And that's why we have won all these finals, because when we get to there, we know that's the only game. There is no other game. There's no other time. And you go down in history. The home finals are probably the moments I remember the most. There's that positive vibe that hits you in the stadium. It's magnetic. It just hits you right there in the tunnel. And it hits the other team in a negative way.

This is a small market—not much attention, not many TV games. So we had to earn it. We made it to being on national TV a lot because of the way we played as a team and because of the stadium. The fans created that. The fans made that. The fans said, "We're going to show up and support the team, and we're going to have that connection with the players, and they're going to see us." I'll always remember the double rainbow before the 2012 Open Cup Final. There weren't always two rainbows over our games. Not even half a rainbow at the beginning. And so I take so much pride when I see rainbows over the sky and everything now.

I'm happy that I've spent more than a decade at this club. Not many people can say that. I've spent the majority of my career here. And it's because everything has been perfect. That's it. Perfect, because I have been able to improve both as a human being and as a player. I love the town and I've grown as a man. I've made a lot of friendships.

2012 U.S. Open Cup
2015 U.S. Open Cup
2017 U.S. Open Cup

Roger Espinoza earned MLS All-Star recognition in 2012 before joining Wigan Athletic of the English Premier League, where he won the 2013 FA Cup. Internationally, Espinoza logged 53 appearances for the Honduras Men's National Team and represented his country at the 2010 and 2014 FIFA World Cups, as well as the 2012 Summer Olympics.

CHILDREN'S MERCY PARK
2011- PRESENT

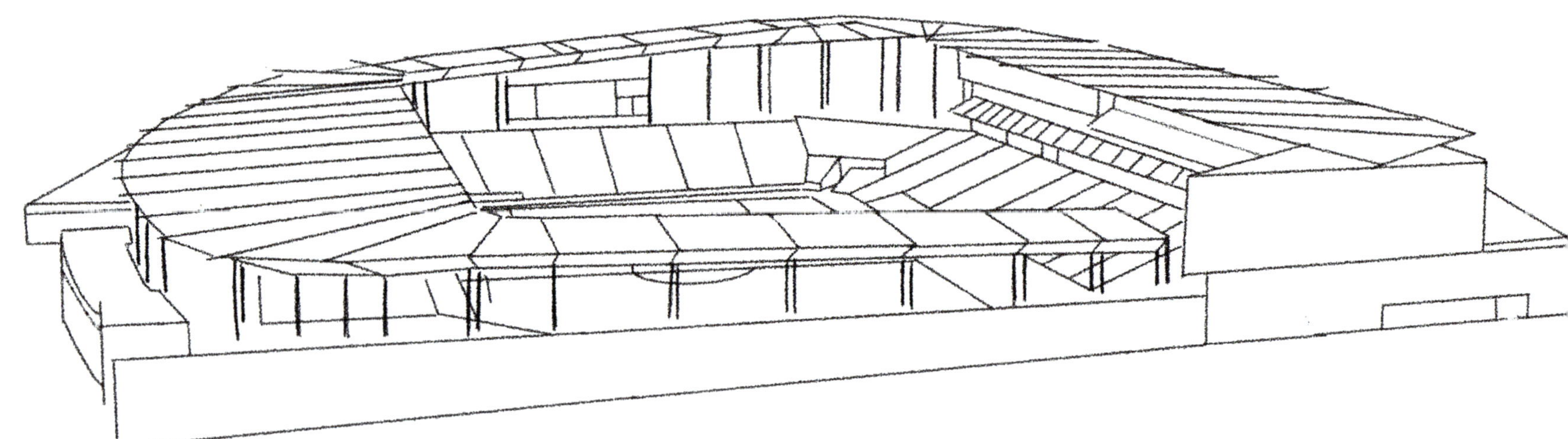

18,467
STADIUM CAPACITY

19,378
AVERAGE ATTENDANCE

86-33-43
RECORD [W-L-T]

"Every time I go to Children's Mercy Park, I dress up, because that's like my temple, my religion. I would say I dress well because I want to feel important, because to me, that place is very important. I mean, that's the place where I forget about everything else completely. Everything—good Lord—nothing goes through my mind. I want to play and I want to be out there because I know that one day I won't be playing, I'll be watching. So for me, every game, every day is is like my last game."

—ROGER ESPINOZA

BENNY FEILHABER #10
adidas
MLS

MY STORY: BENNY FEILHABER

I was told I had been traded to Sporting Kansas City at my bachelor party in Las Vegas, a week before I got married in late 2012. So it was a good pre-wedding gift. I went into my first season in KC with the mindset that I had to perform at a high level in order to continue my playing career. I knew Peter Vermes from my time with the U.S. U-20s when he was one of our assistant coaches. I knew Sporting was one of the better teams in the league, I liked their style of play, and I liked where I could fit into the team.

I played at Sporting Park two or three times while playing for the New England Revolution. It was an awesome stadium, and I really enjoyed playing there. That was another reason why I wanted to come to Kansas City. If you compared Sporting Park with Gillette Stadium, it was night and day.

One of my first days in KC, Peter called me into his office and told me, "Every single person who works for this club and organization has the same goal: to get the team as prepared as possible to get three points on the weekend." That struck a chord with me, because it made me feel like part of something bigger. You feel like you have that support system. That was really special, and it also gave me an added responsibility as a player.

The game-winning goal against Houston in the 2013 Eastern Conference Championship that Dom Dwyer scored off my pass is still what I consider to be my best assist of all time. And I'm sure Dom would say it's one of the better goals he has scored. It's not one of those bangers that he's used to scoring, but the quality of his run, his first touch, the chop back and the simplicity of the finish makes it one of the best goals I've ever been a part of. The celebration and the pandemonium on that play sticks out vividly. Dom's running and doing flips, I'm hugging Graham Zusi, and Paulo Nagamura is kneeling near the corner flag. You could just see from the celebration how much that moment meant to us.

Thinking back to the 2013 MLS Cup against Real Salt Lake, it's crazy. If you look at replays of Lovel Palmer taking RSL's last penalty kick, the ball really does move from the spot right before he kicks it. You wonder, "Man, had it not moved, would that have gone just under the crossbar and into the goal?" We'll never know. It smacked the crossbar, giving us the championship, and everyone reacted pretty quickly. I was one of the last ones to react, because I wasn't sure if the ball had crossed the goal line after hitting the crossbar. If you look at Jimmy Nielsen's face, he had a similar reaction as the goalkeeper. Did the ball go in or out? But it was a truly special moment. Most of the guys on that team had never experienced that kind of championship feeling. For nine or 10 months, you work your butt off to be able to get there. You need to take the right approach as a team but also have some luck. Everything came together for us.

The 2015 season was special for me individually, because I had never played at the level I did that year. We ended up advancing to the Lamar Hunt U.S. Open Cup Final against the Philadelphia Union and, once again, won on penalty kicks. That game was on the road in Philly, and the one thing I remember most was how many Sporting fans were there. We were able to celebrate with maybe 1,000 Sporting fans after we won the game. That was an unbelievable moment, and it meant a lot for me to be able to win a trophy the same year that I had my best individual season.

Now that I have returned to Sporting as a member of the club's technical staff, I think it's very evident that Kansas City is where my soccer family is. This is my opportunity to give back to the players, coaches and fans who supported me during my time as a player.

2013 MLS Cup
2015 U.S. Open Cup
2017 U.S. Open Cup

Benny Feilhaber earned 44 caps for the United States Men's National Team and represented the U.S. at the 2008 Olympics and 2010 FIFA World Cup. Named U.S. Soccer's Player of the Year in 2005, Feilhaber was awarded U.S. Soccer's Best Goal in 2007. His standout 2015 season for Sporting earned him MLS All-Star, MLS Best XI, team MVP and MLS MVP finalist accolades.

Pre-match pageantry prior to kickoff of the 2013 MLS Cup.

THE RISING

THE SEASON IT ALL CAME TOGETHER

The momentum was palpable.

Riding the waves of a transformative rebrand, a freshly minted stadium, a reinvigorated fanbase and a vastly improved team on the field, Sporting Kansas City stormed into 2013 on an upward trajectory. The club had captured the imagination of a tightknit city desperate for championships while making meaningful inroads in the community by connecting with a growing swath of supporters through numerous events and local partnerships.

The foundations were laid, the seeds planted. Less than a decade removed from a turbulent crossroads in which MLS nearly relocated the Wizards to another market, Kansas City was ready to shine as an epicenter of the soccer world. In 2011, the rechristened Sporting climbed from last place to first place in the Eastern Conference. In 2012, fans were treated to the club's first major trophy in eight years as Sporting hoisted the Lamar Hunt U.S. Open Cup and again finished first in the East.

In 2013, the stars aligned like never before.

Hosting one blockbuster event after another, and with Sporting pegged as a genuine title contender, Kansas City was christened as the Soccer Capital of America in what felt like a yearlong celebration.

Chance Myers and Sporting suffered heartbreaking defeat to the Houston Dynamo in the 2012 MLS Cup Playoffs.

PAINT THE WALL

The euphoric highs of 2013 were rooted in adversity.

In an eerily quiet Sporting locker room, media members gathered around goalkeeper and club captain Jimmy Nielsen, whose team had just dominated the Houston Dynamo to win 1-0 in leg two of the Eastern Conference Semifinals at Sporting Park. The result wasn't enough. Having lost the first leg by a 2-0 scoreline in Houston, Sporting was eliminated from the 2012 MLS Cup Playoffs on aggregate.

For the second straight year, an experienced and savvy Dynamo side had inflicted postseason heartbreak on top-seeded Sporting.

"Does this season feel like a disappointment, Jimmy?"

Nielsen paused before answering the reporter's question and considered all that had gone on in 2012—the Lamar Hunt U.S Open Cup title, the 18-7-9 record and first-place finish in the East, the sellout streak already established at Sporting Park.

"No, we have achieved a lot this year," said Nielsen, whose words could be heard by each of his teammates in the oval locker room. "But we are a young team that is still learning and improving. We are going to do everything we possibly can to put ourselves in the same position next year, and when we do, we will take the next step. We don't want to feel this feeling again."

Manager Peter Vermes remembered that evening like a bad dream. The series against Houston was lost in the first leg on the road. Trailing 1-0 in the second half, Sporting became stretched in a frantic bid for an equalizer, and a defensive mistake allowed the Dynamo to double their lead—a lead that proved insurmountable despite Sporting outshooting Houston 20-3 in the second leg at home.

"If you were in the locker room after that game, you instantly understood that not much needed to be said to motivate the guys for the new season," Vermes said.

As with any new season, Sporting experienced a few notable roster changes during the winter months. All-Star midfielder Roger Espinoza, fresh off his best MLS campaign yet and a series of dazzling performances with Honduras at the 2012 Summer Olympics, moved across the Atlantic to sign for English Premier League club Wigan Athletic. Following him to England was the team's top scoring forward, as Sporting loaned Kei Kamara to Norwich City until May.

The sizable returning cast, however, suggested that Sporting would continue to punch with the MLS heavyweights in 2013. Nielsen, who wore the armband with a vibrant and outspoken demeanor, was the reigning MLS Goalkeeper of the Year. In defense, Aurelien Collin was the extravagant and ultra-aggressive yin to Matt Besler's heady and mild-mannered yang. Flanked by indefatigable outside backs Chance Myers and Seth Sinovic, they formed the stingiest backline partnership in MLS.

Graham Zusi, an MLS MVP finalist, was a versatile contributor to the club's dynamic attack alongside youthful forwards Teal Bunbury, C.J. Sapong and Dom Dwyer. In the midfield, grizzled veteran Paulo Nagamura, silky-smooth Spaniard Oriol Rosell and utility men Lawrence Olum and Jacob Peterson were all valuable pieces of the puzzle.

Most importantly, Sporting had cultivated a team-first culture. Players checked their egos at the door, fully committed to their respective roles within a high-pressing, 4-3-3 system designed to dominate possession, suffocate opponents and win the ball back the second it was lost.

"I played professional soccer for 20 years," said Nielsen. "I had experienced some good locker rooms and some bad locker rooms, and then I experienced the Sporting KC locker room. It was something special."

Looking to bolster an offense that sometimes struggled to break defensive bunkers in 2012, Sporting signed prolific Argentine striker Claudio Bieler, a Copa Libertadores champion at Ecuadorian side LDU Quito. Vermes also negotiated within MLS, acquiring two key players via trades on back-to-back days. On Dec. 11, 2012, U.S. international and World Cup veteran Benny Feilhaber joined from the New England Revolution. Some 24 hours later, center back Ike Opara arrived from the San Jose Earthquakes to strengthen an already solid defense.

"In the back of my mind, I knew this might be the last chance I had to prove myself as a player," Feilhaber said. "I wanted to go to a winning club where I could develop and have a good chance to be successful. Sporting checked those boxes."

As the start of the 2013 campaign approached, Vermes caught hold of a Sporting marketing slogan and reinforced the message in numerous discussions with his team. Paint the wall.

The wall, of course, was the northwest corner of Sporting Park where Sporting proudly displayed the years of its four major trophies to date: the 2000 MLS Cup and Supporters' Shield and the 2004 and 2012 U.S. Open Cups. Adding to that collection was the top priority.

Sporting opened the season securing a 3-1 road win over the Philadelphia Union as Zusi, Rosell and MLS debutant Bieler bagged goals. A few weeks later, Sporting picked up its first of five consecutive clean sheets—a miserly run that saw opponents muster just six total shots on target.

On the opposite end of the pitch, Bieler was enjoying a sizzling start to life in MLS with six goals through his first 10 appearances, and Kamara had returned from his loan spell—just in time for a mouthwatering fixture against the bright orange thorn in Sporting's side.

RIVALRIES RENEWED

BBVA Stadium was exactly one year old, still glistening as new on the outskirts of downtown Houston. The Dynamo had protected their new home like a fortress, boasting a 17-0-7 record at the venue and an MLS-record 36-game home unbeaten streak which dated back to the club's earlier days at Robertson Stadium.

May 12 was the one-year anniversary of BBVA Stadium's opening and the first meeting of the regular season between Sporting and Houston. For the visitors, it represented a golden opportunity to set a different tone heading into the summer months.

"We knew that if we wanted to be a championship team, we had to beat Houston at some point," Nagamura said. "That was the only way we could take the next step and reach the level."

In a slugfest that produced 35 fouls compared to 21 shots, Sporting and Houston carried a scoreless stalemate into the second half. At the 73-minute mark, Sinovic heaved a long, looping throw-in from the left sideline into the penalty area. Rising above the rest was Collin, an aerial menace whose close

Graham Zusi and Sporting broke Houston's MLS-record 36-game home unbeaten streak on May 12, 2013.

friend from Houston happened to be in the stands wearing Sporting blue. The Frenchman nodded the ball on with the back of his head, beating Dynamo goalkeeper Tally Hall to seal Sporting's 1-0 triumph.

Houston's historic home unbeaten run, after 694 days, was toast.

"The regular season win over Houston was a key moment psychologically," Assistant Coach Kerry Zavagnin said. "That set the stage for the turning of the tide. Mentally, we knew we could go down there and get a result if we met again in the playoffs."

The springtime Houston encounter was one of two fiercely contested road victories to foreshadow the pulsating playoff drama that awaited.

On July 20, the first-place teams in the East and West squared off as Sporting visited Real Salt Lake in a marquee matchup at Rio Tinto Stadium. By then, the clubs had developed a slowly simmering rivalry that would soon hit a boiling point. The rivalry did not stem from close geography or longstanding history. Its organic origins dated back to a flashbulb moment from two years earlier.

On March 8, 2011, Sporting and RSL met at Reach 11 Sports Complex in Phoenix for a preseason friendly—although nothing about that fateful night was friendly. An increasingly chippy battle melted into mayhem when Espinoza, minutes after his Sporting teammate had suffered a crunching foul, demolished RSL star midfielder Javier Morales just a few feet from the RSL bench. Espinoza was immediately engulfed by a slew of furious Salt Lake players and coaches. In the blink of an eye, a field-storming brawl involving over 20 members of both clubs erupted like searing volcano.

Intending to get involved himself, Nielsen raced out from between the posts and was five yards from the expletive-laced melee when he heard someone call his name. Nielsen turned around and saw RSL goalkeeper Nick Rimando standing alone at midfield.

"I was thinking, 'Is Nicky for real right now?' He wanted to fight me?" Nielsen recalled. "I would have eaten him for breakfast."

Nielsen approached Rimando with swagger. "What's up?"

Rimando had a smirk on his face. "Let's just stand here and watch."

"You know what?" Nielsen replied. "I think that's a great idea."

In that moment, Nielsen and Rimando witnessed the birth of an MLS rivalry that would get nastier and nastier in the seasons that followed. From Sporting's perspective, there was no love lost for the likes of Morales, Kyle Beckerman, Will Johnson, Jamison Olave, Alvaro Saborio, Ned Grabavoy and Chris Wingert. RSL reciprocated the dislike.

Fast-forward two years to a sweltering, 97-degree summer night in Sandy, Utah, and the rivalry's cast of characters hadn't changed much. Espinoza was no longer with Sporting at the time, but the demonstrative Feilhaber had joined the fray as a chief instigator of animosity.

"I always felt that Salt Lake thought they played some kind of superior football and played it better than anyone else," Feilhaber said. "They just had that aura about them. They had achieved some great things as a team, but at the same time I was like, 'Come on, you guys aren't that special.'"

RSL drew first blood in the 56th minute through Robbie Findley, but the hosts were reduced to 10 men shortly after when Wingert received a red card for his second bookable offense of the night. Seconds later, Sporting restored parity as 20-year-old Soony Saad finished off a pass from Bieler.

With a man advantage, Sporting grew in stature and pushed forward in search of the winner. In the seventh minute of second-half stoppage time, with RSL coaches and fans clamoring for the full-time whistle, Sporting was awarded a corner kick. As Zusi trotted toward the flag to take the set piece, he did something he always made sure to do prior to taking a free kick. He crossed paths with Opara.

Excellent in the air and a major threat on set

Ike Opara's dramatic 97th-minute match-winner after a chippy affair against Real Salt Lake at Rio Tinto Stadium, July 20, 2013, fueled the rivalry.

pieces, Opara muttered words only Zusi could hear: "Near post, Zus."

"At that point," Zusi said, "all my concentration was trying to put the ball where Ike could get to it."

Zusi whipped an inch-perfect corner into the mixer with his sights set on Opara, who shook free of Aaron Maund, skipped toward the near post and snapped a bouncing header into the corner of the net for the latest goal in Kansas City's regular season history. With a mosh pit piling on Opara near the visitors' bench, Sporting had prevailed 2-1 to claim three crucial points in the Supporters' Shield race.

"It was a massive win for us—one of those that you just wanted to keep celebrating inside that stadium," Zusi said. "We had knocked off a team we didn't like very much and solidified ourselves as one of the teams to beat moving forward."

STAR TREATMENT

At the end of July, Kansas City was given a platform to showcase itself as a premier market in Major League Soccer. On paper, the 2013 MLS All-Star Game against Italian club AS Roma was the headline event. The electric four-day period that preceded it, though, resonated just as powerfully as a midsummer celebration of the sport in Kansas City.

In the space of 96 hours, as a 30-foot inflatable All-Star jersey toured popular destinations across the metro, the Kansas City Power & Light District hosted two free concerts—Macklemore and Ryan Lewis on July 29 and the Silversun Pickups on July 30—plus a 5K jersey run and a fashion event in which Collin unveiled his own AC78 clothing line.

"Kansas City is a place that is very authentic and genuine," Collin said. "If you show the people that you're doing everything in your power to serve the city and to be a good representation of the club on and off the field, they will embrace you. The love I received there was like nowhere else. That is why I still call Kansas City home."

Collin spent part of All-Star Week painting the town red with one of the world's most famous athletes. Linking up with French soccer legend and fellow All-Star Thierry Henry, Collin took his countryman to some of his favorite spots—Westport Café, Tannin Wine Bar and Fogo de Chao.

A festive audience of 21,175 filled Sporting Park for the All-Star Game on the final day of July. Vermes, the All-Star team's head coach, delighted Sporting fans by giving starts to Collin, Besler and Zusi. A formidable Roma team featuring U.S. international Michael Bradley and Italian legend Francesco Totti won 3-1, but the result was inconsequential: Kansas City had knocked All-Star week out of the park.

ROUNDING INTO FORM

That same week, Feilhaber was in full stride, sweating through his training top and nearing the end of an intense run. He wasn't training at Swope Soccer Village, surrounded by teammates and coaches. He was grinding on a treadmill at a fitness center in the nearby suburb of Overland Park, surrounded by families and amateur bodybuilders.

Feilhaber hated running. He readily admitted, "Fitness was never my thing," but in order to thrive in Vermes' high-pressing system—one predicated on extreme physical exertion—he needed to be in better shape.

Having lost his starting spot in June, Feilhaber was assigned to extra fitness work in a bid to become "Sporting fit"—the term widely used to describe the team's superior conditioning. Relegating him to

The 2013 MLS All-Star Game at Sporting Park was a spectacle. Matt Besler, Graham Zusi and Aurelien Collin all started for the MLS All-Stars, managed by Peter Vermes.

Benny Feilhaber led Sporting to victory over the New England Revolution, his former club, in the 2013 Eastern Conference Semifinals.

the bench, Vermes made it clear to Feilhaber that his work rate on the defensive side of the ball also needed to improve.

"Between me being an ass to Benny in that moment and then the bench being his best coach, all of those things intertwined to grab his attention," Vermes said. "By playoff time, he had latched on to how important it was to be able to transition from offense to defense and immediately put pressure on the other team when we didn't have the ball."

Feilhaber's quality in the final third was undeniable. Sporting's demanding style of play, however, meant that Feilhaber spent large portions of 2013 in assimilation mode. He was often used as a sub from May to July and didn't even play in three of the team's last four regular season matches or the first leg of the Eastern Conference Semifinals against New England.

Sporting ended the regular season the same way they started it, prevailing on the road in Philadelphia. A breathless 2-1 win over the Union on Oct. 26 temporarily lifted Sporting into pole position for the Supporters' Shield, rounding out a 17-10-7 record, but the Red Bulls stole the regular season title by hammering Chicago the following day.

"The Supporters' Shield would have been amazing to win, but it wasn't our main goal," Nagamura said. "If anything, the way the regular season ended made us even hungrier for the playoffs."

THE TRANSITION MOMENT

Close to midnight, Vermes and Collin had gathered for drinks at the hotel bar in Foxborough, Massachusetts. A few hours earlier, Sporting had fallen 2-1 to New England in the first leg of the Eastern Conference Semifinals. The Revolution briefly held a two-goal lead midway through the second half before Sporting grabbed one back through Collin.

"That goal was massive; keeps us in it," Vermes told Collin. "And I guarantee you, when we go back to Kansas City, we're winning this thing and we're moving to the next round."

Collin, like most of his teammates, was fuming after the match. Not only did the 2-1 scoreline flatter New England, but the Revs' team celebration after Kelyn Rowe scored the second goal of the night was, in the opinion of many in the Sporting contingent, excessively brash. It wouldn't be forgotten.

Vermes had a few lineup changes planned for leg two. Nagamura, nursing an ankle injury and held out for the first leg on New England's field turf, would join the midfield. So, too, would Feilhaber, who had played just once in Sporting's previous five games.

With the stakes higher than ever, Feilhaber was on the brink of his best performance yet in a Sporting uniform. Packed to the gills for the return leg on Nov. 6, Sporting Park shook with postseason energy as Sporting seized attacking initiative. Collin would strike again on the cusp of halftime, leveling the aggregate score at 2-2.

"I still don't understand it, but I think God gave me scoring abilities in the playoffs," said Collin, who would eventually finish as the leading scorer of the 2013 postseason. "I had never scored that many goals in my whole life."

The Revolution responded in the 70th minute to reclaim a one-goal cushion on aggregate and put Sporting behind the eight-ball. Dominant from start to finish that night—Sporting outshot New England

32-5 with Feilhaber and Zusi creating six scoring chances each—the hosts were staring down the barrel of another abrupt playoff exit.

With 78 minutes on the clock, Collin floated a long, searching ball toward the edge of the Revolution penalty area. Zusi, not one who prided himself on aerial duels, outjumped his marker to flick the ball into the path of an on-running Sinovic, who sent a thunderous blast into the far corner—a sublime strike from a left back who had scored once previously in his MLS career.

"Seth could not have hit this ball any better if he tried a million times," Zusi said. "One of the greatest goals in Sporting history from a guy who didn't score much."

Sinovic's headfirst slide at the corner flag, just a few feet away from the manic Cauldron, became a vintage celebration in club folklore. More significantly, his goal had restored parity on aggregate to set up 30 minutes of extra time.

"In the 2011 and 2012 playoffs, I remember feeling hope but also stress and anxiety," Zavagnin said. "There was a slight fear within the group. When Seth scored that goal, you could feel it in the stadium—the way everyone reacted to that play, the stress and anxiety were gone."

The extra-time session belonged to the two players that Sporting acquired before the season specifically to provide a cutting edge in attack. In the 113th minute, Feilhaber made a game-winning defensive play in a transition moment—executing precisely what Vermes had preached all year long—by intercepting a long outlet throw from New England goalkeeper Matt Reis. He then accelerated down the right side, entered the box and squared to Bieler, who made good on Sporting's Designated Player investment with a cool finish past Reis to seal a gripping 4-3 aggregate victory.

"If it wasn't for what I went through earlier that year, I never would have been able to see that play and act on it," Feilhaber said. "It was exactly what the team needed of me and it finally clicked in my brain. That play was the perfect example of what it took for me to become a really important player for Kansas City."

Once again within touching distance of the MLS Cup, Sporting had to clear one more hurdle. A third straight playoff battle with Houston—and a shot at sweet revenge—beckoned on the horizon.

OVER THE HUMP

In a cagey first leg of the Eastern Conference Championship at Houston, Nielsen leapt to snag an incoming cross and felt the brunt of Houston attacker Will Bruin's aerial challenge.

Just like that, two broken ribs. It left Nielsen in serious pain, needing help from his wife just to get out of bed.

The good news? Nielsen and Sporting had earned a shutout in leg one at BBVA Stadium, bringing the series back to Kansas City tied 0-0 on aggregate. A year earlier, Sporting returned home from Houston in a 2-0 hole.

Additionally, Nielsen had two full weeks to recover for the second leg on Nov. 23. He took pain

Aurelien Collin made a colossal impact with a league-leading three goals during the 2013 MLS Cup Playoffs.

medicine every day to ease the discomfort in his midsection and was severely limited in practice, conducting basic handling drills and not much else. Even so, Vermes was banking on the 36-year-old to be available on matchday.

"I never had a doubt he was playing," Vermes said. "Jimmy never allowed his injury to come to my attention. There was no way he was ever going to put a doubt in my mind of whether or not he could play. That's the type of competitor he was."

The Saturday before Thanksgiving, a stadium-record 21,650 supporters converged on Sporting Park with temperatures hovering around 22 degrees. The atmosphere was fitting for a final, but Houston landed a sucker punch within three minutes to take air out of the crowd. Boniek Garcia's close-range shot took a fortuitous deflection and skipped past Nielsen, who was wearing a vest under his pink goalkeeper jersey to protect his ribs.

"We fall behind quickly and for a split second, you think, 'Oh no, not again,'" Nielsen said.

Sporting's timely response worked wonders to settle the nerves of players and spectators alike. In the 14th minute, Feilhaber dribbled purposefully into a swarm of Houston defenders on the edge of the box. His pressure forced an errant touch from Dynamo defender Bobby Boswell, giving Sapong a clean look to equalize with a right-footed laser.

"In that moment, you felt it," Feilhaber said. "We weren't the same team as we were in 2011 and 2012. Speed bumps weren't going to prevent us from going where we wanted to go."

Sporting and Houston remained deadlocked until the hour mark, when Feilhaber and Dwyer combined to unlock the Dynamo defense in jaw-dropping fashion.

Dribbling the ball in his own half, Nagamura squeezed an incisive pass across midfield to Zusi, who beat one defender and found Feilhaber in a pocket of space. Seeing his opening, Feilhaber surged to the top of the box and scooped an impudent, waist-high pass that eluded the touch of two Dynamo players and landed at the feet of Dwyer. The striker took a velvety first touch and slotted home as Sporting Park roared in ecstasy.

Dom Dwyer's dramatic winner against Houston in the 2013 Eastern Conference Championship is one of the most iconic goals in club history.

"That's what I consider to be my best assist of all time," Feilhaber said. "It's literally poetry in motion. Everyone knows what's about to happen, but Houston can't do anything about it."

Sporting protected a 2-1 lead until full time, heaving the Houston-sized monkey off their backs and advancing to the MLS Cup on Dec. 7. Major League Soccer's championship match would be played at Sporting Park, the biggest professional championship game in Kansas City since the 1985 World Series.

"We knew that the Houston game was the one we needed to get past," Nagamura said. "Once we got over the hump, you didn't want to get overconfident, but it was a special feeling knowing that MLS Cup was right here in our own backyard."

DREAMS COME TRUE IN SPORTING BLUE

It wasn't bulletin board material. It was television screen material.

A few days before Sporting hosted Real Salt Lake in the MLS Cup, Vermes gathered players, coaches and support staff inside the meeting room at Swope Soccer Village. He had asked his staff to prepare a video, except this one was far different than his typical scouting reports.

The video began with remarks from RSL general manager Garth Lagerwey, a former goalkeeper for the Kansas City Wiz in 1996.

"We want to keep the ball, we want to possess, we want to attack," Lagerwey told sports blog Grantland the week after RSL suffered its last-gasp home loss to Sporting. "Kansas City wants to kick people, pressure you all over the field, and try to rely on set pieces and turnovers to generate their chances."

He continued: "Kansas City leads the league in fouls committed by a wide margin. They wear their style on their sleeve. They're going to come in and try and intimidate and impose their style and even beat you up a little bit. They're not shy about that, they're proud of it. So I think the league has to decide: do they want that kind of physical, rock'em-sock'em style, or do they want to play more of a passing, possession, beautiful game?"

The video then transitioned to a montage of Sporting's best highlights throughout the season—wonderfully worked team goals, intricate passing sequences and quickfire counterattacks. Various statistics popped up on the screen, pointing out that Sporting not only led MLS in average possession and chances created, but also had five fewer red cards than RSL that year. Lagerwey's perception didn't seem to match reality.

Needless to say, this particular film session had its desired effect.

"I didn't have to do a lot of motivating after that video," Vermes said.

On the morning of Saturday, Dec. 7, Vermes arrived at Sporting Park for the biggest match of his coaching career. Dressed in layers, he marched through a stadium tunnel and onto the pitch. Bright rays of sunshine did nothing to cut through the numbing freeze that had swallowed Kansas City that weekend. With temperatures plummeting near zero degrees overnight, segments of the playing surface on the shade-covered south end of the field were completely frozen.

"If that was a regular season game," Vermes said, "it probably would have been called off."

Players entered valet parking near the stadium loading dock at 1:30 p.m., roughly 90 minutes before 3 p.m. kickoff. By then, temperatures had eclipsed 10 degrees and the entire Members Stand was full.

By 2:30, a record-equaling crowd of 21,650 had assembled for the most consequential match in Sporting's 18-year existence. Supporters of all ages, enveloped in winter jackets and championship scarves, brandished flags and rally towels while yelling and chanting in full voice.

"When we walked onto the field for warmups and saw the stadium completely full, I thought, what a moment," Nielsen said. "What a reward to the city to be able to host a final in this stadium. These fans deserve every bit of this."

Every exhale was visible from the 22 players on the hardened pitch as referee Hilario Grajeda whistled the start of what would become an instant classic and, at the time, the coldest MLS game on record. Unfortunately for Sporting, the first setback came after just eight minutes when Rosell, the invaluable holding midfielder, sprained his left ankle and was forced to exit. He was replaced by Olum,

Despite freezing temperatures, the Eastern Conference Championship and MLS Cup in 2013 welcomed stadium-record crowds of 21,650 fans at Sporting Park.

Aurelien Collin scored Sporting's all-important equalizer and converted an inch-perfect penalty kick in the MLS Cup. He was named MVP of the match.

who had not seen action in a month since fracturing his fibula.

What Olum lacked in speed and technical quality he made up for with sheer calmness and composure. With a relaxed disposition and an ability to approach the sternest of challenges with utmost poise, Olum was up for the task.

"If there was one guy you wanted to enter the game at that moment—someone who wasn't expecting to play and was suddenly called upon to play pretty much the whole game—it was Olum," Zavagnin said.

As the game ebbed and flowed, Nielsen struggled to find his footing. The six-yard boxes had essentially become ice patches, which made for near-unplayable goalkeeping conditions. Nielsen had his heart in his mouth on two occasions, first when Findley's shot rattled the post and caromed into his thankful hands at the half-hour mark and again in the second half when Morales chipped the keeper only to see his effort ping off the post, trickle agonizingly across the goalmouth and roll wide.

Seven minutes after the restart, Saborio silenced the crowd by firing RSL ahead 1-0. For the third straight time in the 2013 playoffs, Sporting had conceded first. And for the third straight time, their response was superb.

"We never panicked," Nagamura said. "So what if we fell behind? It happened in the conference semifinals. It happened in the conference finals. It happened in MLS Cup. We were too strong to fall under the pressure."

In the 76th minute, Sporting earned a corner kick in front of the lively but increasingly anxious Cauldron. Zusi scurried to the flag and placed the ball carefully, hoping it would sit up nicely in a frozen area of the field.

"I was ultra-focused on just being able to kick the ball and not fall on my butt or send it into the Cauldron," Zusi said. "My only aim was trying to put the ball in a semi-dangerous spot."

What happened next was nothing short of monumental. Zusi curled his corner into a congested penalty area and Collin began to time his jump. As the ball reached its zenith, the 6-foot-2 Frenchman bodied 6-foot-4 RSL defender Chris Schuler and took off on a towering vertical leap near the penalty spot. Stationed in goal, Rimando could only flap at Collin's colossal header.

Sporting 1, Real Salt Lake 1.

"That goal," Collin said, "was the greatest moment in my humble career."

Rocking with belief, supporters willed Sporting into second-half stoppage time and 30 minutes of nerve-frying extra time, but nothing could separate the sides. The 2013 MLS Cup would be decided by penalty kicks.

Calm and confident, Vermes and the technical staff huddled with players on the sideline and hashed out the order of Sporting's first five penalty takers. Feilhaber knew then and there that he would be sending his attempt straight down the middle. Nagamura planned to make a last-second read on Rimando before picking a corner.

Nielsen, meanwhile, was ready to play head games in what became a 10-round nail-biter in front of the riotous Cauldron.

After Bieler buried his attempt to put Sporting up 1-0, Nielsen approached the goalmouth with three pieces of paper in his mitts. Was it a cheat sheet? What did Nielsen know about Saborio's PK history? Surely those questions lingered in the RSL forward's mind as he prepared to take his team's first penalty. Nielsen glanced at the sheets until Saborio was ready to strike, then cast them aside as the Costa Rican smashed his shot over the crossbar. Advantage to Sporting.

Nagamura sunk his penalty to make it 2-0 and motioned three emphatic fist bumps to the Cauldron. Next, Nielsen took another cursory look at his papers. One contained a scribbled note from Sporting goalkeeper coach John Pascarella. "Just like Seattle" it read with a smiley face.

Nielsen, looking to duplicate his shootout heroics from the 2012 Lamar Hunt U.S. Open Cup Final versus Seattle, dove right to save Ned Grabavoy's penalty.

From there, however, RSL settled into a rhythm. Following Rimando's save on Besler, RSL sank five consecutive penalties while Zusi saw his would-be game-winner sail high in the fifth round. With the score tied at 5-5 entering the eighth frame, Olum pulled his shot wide. Sebastian Velasquez would have a chance to win it for RSL.

As the 22-year-old stepped to the spot, Nielsen employed some positive self-talk. Whether or not Velasquez could hear him amid the roar of the stadium, he did not know.

"I know where your last three shots have been and I know where you're going again."

Velasquez went to the goalkeeper's left. So did Nielsen, palming the ball aside to keep Sporting alive.

Myers and RSL defender Nat Borchers traded successful kicks in the ninth round. Nielsen then tried to get the attention of Sporting's technical staff. He desperately wanted to go tenth. Or perhaps he desperately didn't want Collin to go tenth.

Nevertheless, Collin strode to the spot as Sporting's worst penalty taker. For the first time in the entire shootout, Zavagnin turned away from the action. He couldn't watch.

What Zavagnin missed was the finest penalty in the shootout, as Collin's sweetly struck side-footer nestled inches inside the right post.

Collin's conversion put all of the pressure on RSL's tenth penalty taker, Lovel Palmer.

With over 20,000 home fans yelling their throats dry, the RSL defender smacked his shot off the crossbar. A deafening jolt of euphoria emitted from Sporting Park. Sporting Kansas City were champions of Major League Soccer.

Nielsen raised his arms in triumph. Hordes of teammates sprinted toward him, accidentally trampling Nagamura in the process. Collin began to cry. Zavagnin darted in the general direction of the growing Sporting mob and haphazardly ran into his wife, who had hopped onto the field from the first row in the Cauldron, for a warm hug.

Jimmy Nielsen studied his cheat sheet—which included a motivational note from goalkeeper coach John Pascarella—before the shootout that decided the MLS Cup champion.

On Oct. 1, 2014, the MLS Cup champions visited Washington, D.C. for an honorary ceremony with President Barack Obama at the White House.

"It felt like a celebration of the last three years," said Collin, who joined Sporting after the rebrand in 2011 and was named the 2013 MLS Cup MVP that night. "I cannot even describe the emotion. It was the perfect ending to the best year in my life."

The Philip F. Anschutz trophy had a busy schedule in the celebratory aftermath that followed. It would be raised by Nielsen, Sporting's captain, and passed from one teammate to the next. It would be hoisted by Besler and Zusi near the Cauldron in what became one of the most iconic images in club history. It would make its way into the Sporting locker room for a green screen photo shoot. It would take a dip into Sporting's six-person hot tub—more than 20 players crammed into it at once to thaw out—and it would later serve as a goblet for beer, champagne and other adult beverages.

But before all of that, Sporting's co-owner Robb Heineman hijacked the trophy and took it to the Members' Club where one ecstatic supporter after another caressed the $100,000 prize.

"Our city and our fans deserved that championship," Vermes said. "When you looked around the stadium at everyone who was involved that night—players, staff members, fans, community members—everyone was bought in and fully committed for 120 minutes plus penalties. It was incredibly satisfying to know how far we had come as a club."

Postgame revelry lasted into the early hours of Dec. 8 as Kansas City celebrated its first professional sports championship since the Wizards won the 2000 MLS Cup. Soccer in Kansas City had undergone a radical transformation since then—a transformation that no one could have possibly predicted at the turn of the millennium.

"2013 was a confirmation to the ownership group, the technical staff, the players and the fans," Nagamura said. "We showed that Kansas City was a shining star in MLS."

On Oct. 1, 2014, several months after Sporting blue confetti showered Sporting Park, the MLS Cup champions visited the White House for an honorary celebration. Sporting players, coaches and owners gathered in the East Room to huddle around President Barack Obama, who remarked on the club's storybook accomplishment.

He spoke about Kansas City's love for soccer and Sporting's amazing playoff run. He spoke about the achievements of Vermes and the players. Then he cast light on a simple yet powerful dynamic that had become the very lifeblood of the club.

"In the same way that Kansas City has embraced its soccer team," the President said, "the soccer team has embraced the city."

That embrace is still felt today, and is crucial to the continued connection between the club and the community.

"When you look at the 2013 season," said Zavagnin, "and where it sits in the evolution of our club and the growth of soccer in Kansas City, it's the most significant year we've ever experienced." ♦

SEAL OF THE PRESIDENT OF THE UNITED STATES

MY STORY: MATT BESLER

"In 1996 when the Wiz started, I was 10 years old. As a 10-year-old kid, going to games wasn't so much about the game itself, but rather all the other experiences that come along with attending a game: the vuvuzela horns, the Macarena, the Papa John's Magic Minutes, trying to make it onto the jumbotron, nachos, catching a free T-shirt from Dynamo the Dragon, chanting "Let's Go Wiz!" and then laughing.

It's easy to say now I expected to be drafted. But in all honesty, I had no idea. I was simply hoping to get an opportunity. I spoke with a few teams at the MLS Player Combine, none of which were Kansas City. When Kansas City went on the clock with pick #8, I got butterflies in my stomach; there was still a sliver of hope I held onto that I would somehow end up in my hometown. A few minutes later, Commissioner Don Garber arrived at the podium and said, "With the 8th pick in the 2009 MLS SuperDraft, the Kansas City Wizards select Matt Besler."

Those words will forever live in my head. I don't think anyone truly realized how special it was for me. I tried to explain to others how much I love my hometown, and how proud I am to be from Kansas City, but no one quite understood. The next hour was a blur. Jimmy Conrad, who was the captain at the time, called me to welcome me to the team. I met all the coaches; I met a few of the KC fans who drove over [to St. Louis, site of the draft]. One fan I remember in particular was Deanna Weymuth, and she gave me a bag of her famous chocolate chip cookies.

For me, my first couple seasons were all about survival. Forget about playing, starting, all-star, national team or World Cup. None of that was on my mind. I was simply trying to make the team each year. The way that Peter [Vermes] coached, he clearly had a certain style of play. For the most part, every guy on the team bought in. But if you don't win, it doesn't validate anything. So I think [the 2012] U.S. Open Cup final, that's the reason why it was so big. Because for two years we had been building the style of play. There was a weather delay [lasting 37 minutes] before the game. And I'm telling you, when we finally walked out, I looked around and I was like, "Holy shit, this atmosphere is unbelievable." The buzz, the electricity, the fact that it just rained, and people were already rowdy, and you could just feel that right away. One of the best warm-ups we had there ended up being that unbelievable rainbow right over the stadium during warm-ups, and the players could see it perfectly.

[During the penalty kick shootout,] When Eddie Johnson walked up, there's already a lot of pressure—you could feel it in the stadium. The longer he waited, the louder the stadium got and the tension just kept building. If you were in the stadium, you know exactly what I'm talking about, because every single person in that stadium could feel the exact same thing.

I think that win was not just a turning point in our club's history, I think it also was a turning point in our city's sports history, because I think people walked away from that stadium that night and everyone said the same thing: "This feels amazing; we want more!" That night we gave the city something to be proud of, proud about. And you just saw the effect that it had throughout the city.

It's very rewarding and satisfying to know that you were able to provide special memories for so many people. That's one of the coolest parts about reminiscing on some of these games and accomplishments that we had. It's not only that you create memories for yourself and for your family, but you created memories for so many other Kansas Citians. People coming up to you and saying, "I took my two sons to the game in 2012, and that was one of the best sporting events we've ever been to and we still talk about it to this day."

Hearing stuff like that, I mean, that's the special part about sports, and that's the special part about this club, because so many people are connected in that way.

2012 U.S. Open Cup
2013 MLS Cup
2015 U.S. Open Cup
2017 U.S. Open Cup

Matt Besler was named MLS Defender of the Year in 2012 and earned MLS Best XI honors in 2012 and 2013. A five-time MLS All-Star, Besler captained Sporting from 2014 to 2020 and made 47 caps for the United States Men's National Team, including four appearances at the 2014 FIFA World Cup.

FOR CLUB & COUNTRY

FROM KANSAS CITY TO BRAZIL

Their shared status as Sporting Kansas City legends grew astronomically over the course of two concurrent storylines in 2013.

Matt Besler and Graham Zusi, who fatefully joined the club together as 2009 MLS SuperDraft selections, had become staples of the United States Men's National Team four years later. Dual responsibilities as stars for Sporting and the U.S. would help elevate the duo as two of the country's most recognizable soccer players.

From unproven rookies who lived in Besler's parents' basement in 2009 to breakout performers in 2011 to MLS Best XI honorees and U.S. Open Cup champions in 2012, Besler and Zusi had become pivotal national team contributors under head coach Jurgen Klinsmann.

"Every stepping-stone we took as players, we pretty much took them together," Zusi said. "When I reflect on my career, I'm going to see Matt right there with me."

Early 2013 marked the first time Besler and Zusi were both selected to the USMNT for World Cup qualifying. On March 22, Zusi started as the Americans weathered a blinding Colorado snowstorm to beat Costa Rica 1-0. Four days later, Besler enjoyed his coming-out party for the U.S. with a masterful defensive performance versus archrival Mexico at the fabled Estadio Azteca. Despite the hostility created by 86,000 boisterous spectators and ceaseless pressure applied by Mexican phenoms like Javier "Chicharito" Hernandez and Giovani Dos Santos, the Sporting center back was unflappable.

Besler's faultless display in Mexico City led to increased minutes with the USMNT, including starts in the quarterfinals, semifinals and final of the 2013 Concacaf Gold Cup in mid-July. The Kansas City native was instrumental in the knockout stage, propelling the Yanks to victories over El Salvador, Honduras and Panama as the U.S. won its fifth Gold Cup title.

"Matt rose to the occasion that year," Zusi said. "This was his first experience with the U.S. national team—a massive moment for any player—and he exceeded all expectations. He was just an animal all year long."

The national team excitement surrounding Besler and Zusi reached new heights on Oct. 11 when the U.S., already assured of a berth at the 2014 FIFA World Cup in Brazil, hosted Jamaica in the penultimate matchday of World Cup qualifying at Children's Mercy Park. A win would see the Americans clinch first place in the Hexagonal.

But before Besler and Zusi took the field under the Friday night lights, an equally momentous event took place that afternoon on the Children's Mercy Park plaza. Sporting Manager Peter Vermes, a 1990 World Cup captain for the U.S. and a 2000 MLS Cup champion with the Kansas City Wizards, was formally honored for his playing and coaching excellence as an inductee into the National Soccer Hall of Fame. Donning a bright red U.S. Soccer sport coat, Vermes took the podium to graciously thank everyone—from his parents and siblings in New Jersey to the thousands of supporters in Kansas City—who had helped him become one of the most accomplished figures in American soccer history.

Vermes' induction was the ideal table setter for the nightcap as a throbbing sea of red, white and blue-clad supporters filled Children's Mercy Park. Banners hung, flags waved and chants bellowed from all corners of the venue.

Besler started in central defense, marshalling a U.S. side that comfortably kept Jamaica at bay for all 90 minutes. But with the match tied 0-0 at intermission, the Americans needed a spark. Zusi would provide just that.

Disappointed he hadn't started that night, Zusi replaced Landon Donovan at halftime and took the field to a rousing ovation from the Kansas City faithful. Buzzing from the emotional high of representing his country in Sporting's own stadium, he covered the left flank like a gazelle and wound up conjuring the decisive breakthrough.

In the 77th minute, Zusi latched onto a low cross from Alejandro Bedoya and unfurled a right-footed shot inside the far post as Children's Mercy Park burst into pandemonium.

"It was one of those blackout celebrations where you totally forget what you're doing," said Zusi, who jumped into Besler's widespread arms before a host of other U.S. players joined the warm embrace. The Americans doubled their advantage a few minutes later through Jozy Altidore, coming away with a 2-0 win to wrap up first place in the Hexagonal. Afterward, Zusi was named man of the match for his game-changing, 45-minute cameo.

Several months later, at the 2014 FIFA World Cup in Brazil, Besler and Zusi were integral members of a U.S. side that reached the knockout stages after finishing second in a so-called "group of death" that featured Ghana, Cristiano Ronaldo and Portugal, and eventual champions Germany. Besler started all four matches in the tournament, while Zusi assisted two goals with starts in three of four appearances.

"What Matt and I experienced at the World Cup was probably our high point with the national team," Zusi said. "But that night in Kansas City—winning the Hex and doing it in front of our home fans—those memories are priceless."

Oct. 11, 2013 was a winning night for the Sporting/U.S. contingent, as Peter Vermes was inducted into the National Soccer Hall of Fame, Matt Besler featured in the starting 11 and Graham Zusi subbed on to score the match-winner.

SNAPSHOT
SPORTING
2011 - PRESENT

1) Ball and autographed CJ Sapong boot from first Sporting KC goal at Children's Mercy Park, June 17, 2011.

2) Signed letter from President Barack Obama, thanking the club for their trip to the White House and the thoughtful gifts, Oct. 27, 2014.

3) Editorial cartoon, *Kansas City Star*, 2013: "The Most Powerful Element in Advertising is Truth." Cartoon by Bob Unell.

4) Sporting/Wiz retro pre-match training top featuring 20th anniversary mark and autographed by April 13, 2016, team.

5) Matt Besler "Paint The Wall" bobblehead

6) "Black Lives Matter" captain's armband from 2020 season, with team locker room motto: "From Many Paths, We Become One."

7) Jimmy Nielsen's 2013 MLS Cup penalty kick cheat sheets, featuring "Just like Seattle" note from Goalkeeper Coach John Pascarella.

1

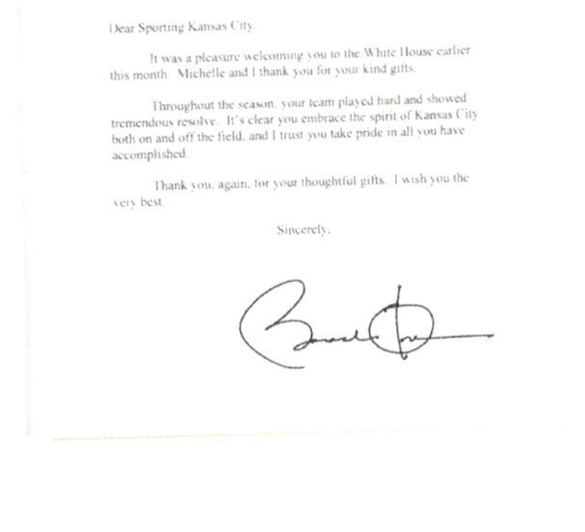

THE WHITE HOUSE
WASHINGTON

October 27, 2014

Sporting Kansas City
1511 Baltimore Avenue
Kansas City, Missouri 64108

Dear Sporting Kansas City:

It was a pleasure welcoming you to the White House earlier this month. Michelle and I thank you for your kind gifts.

Throughout the season, your team played hard and showed tremendous resolve. It's clear you embrace the spirit of Kansas City both on and off the field, and I trust you take pride in all you have accomplished.

Thank you, again, for your thoughtful gifts. I wish you the very best.

Sincerely,

2

3

4

5

6

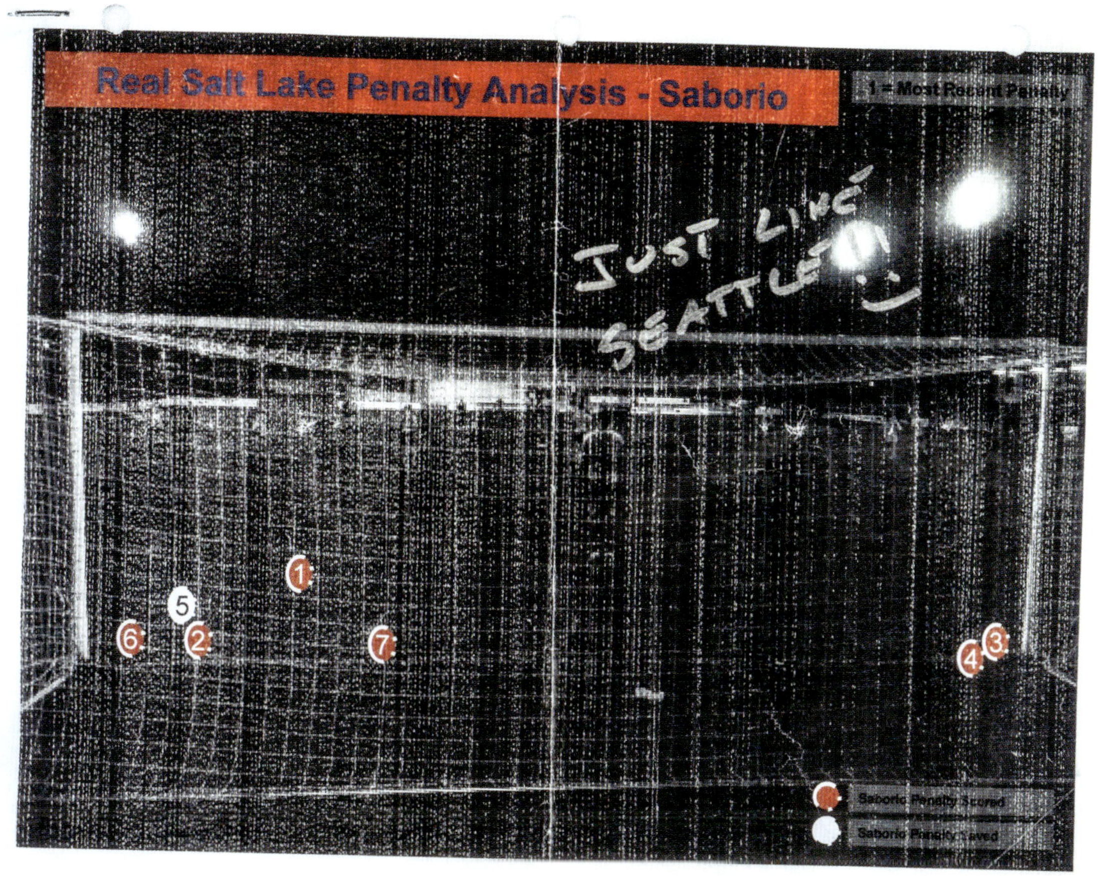

7

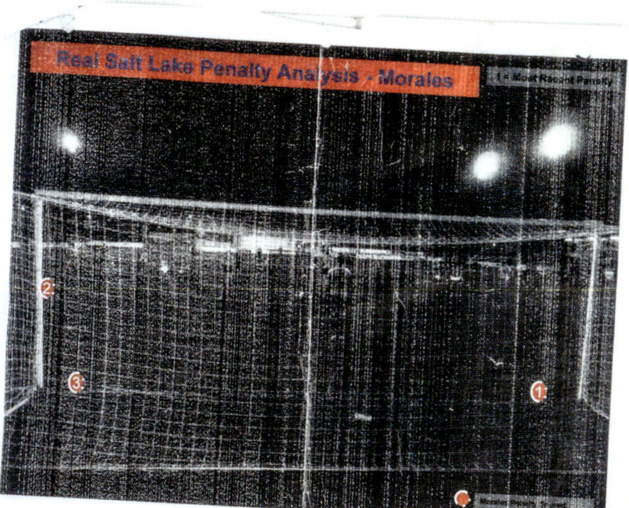

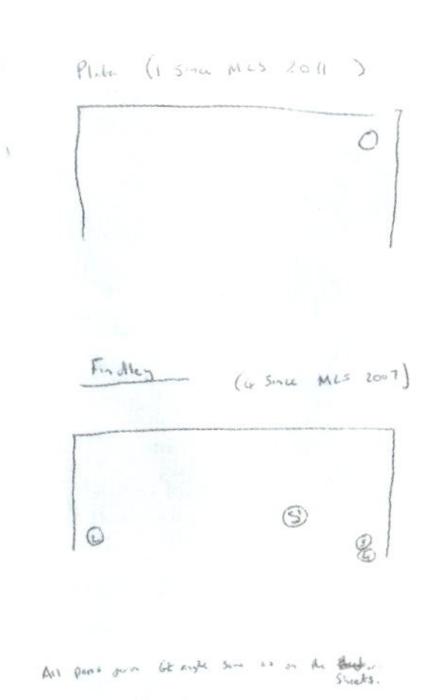

adidas

Real Salt Lake Penalty Analysis - Saborio
1 = Most Recent Penalty
JUST LIKE SEATTLE!!!
1
5
6
2
7
4
3
Saborio Penalty Scored
Saborio Penalty Saved

Real Salt Lake Penalty Analysis - Morales
1 = Most Recent Penalty
2
3
1

Findley
(6 Since MLS 2007)

SPORTING

Ivy
INVESTMENTS

MY STORY: GRAHAM ZUSI

"To be completely honest, I knew very little about Kansas City, other than the fact that a fellow Terp, Abe Thompson, was currently on the team.

I knew that being drafted [in 2009] was no more than basically a tryout. I was in class at that point. I didn't come to Kansas City; my dad came out [to the University of Maryland] and helped me pack from school. And we drove straight to Bradenton, Florida, and met up with the team there.

It was a good group of guys, and I specifically remember Matt Besler as well. We were two of the few rookies who lasted the entire preseason. So Matt and I immediately just kind of formed a bond out of necessity, really. I actually didn't sign a contract until four days before the the season opener.

My first couple of years, I was a role player; I would often come in late in games and try to be a bit of a spark off the bench, if you will. But in terms of the city, I was kind of learning the ins and outs of it. In my first year, I lived in a few different places. Obviously, I think a lot of people know that I ended up in Besler's basement with his family for the remainder of that first year. I was very fortunate to have really good people around me. And the Beslers were gracious enough to bring me into their home and allow a kid who is in a new city, and unfamiliar with that kind of lifestyle, to kind of get his roots in place and really just focus on my soccer.

Probably my most memorable moment at CAB was when I scored my first goal professionally; I look back on what I did as a celebration, and I love every part of it. My instinct was to just jump over the barriers and go and hug the Cauldron. And it was, I guess, a love at first sight moment for me.

I'll never forget the first time we played at Children's Mercy Park. Just the energy and atmosphere that place had from day one was absolutely incredible. I felt zero fatigue or tiredness in that game just because there was so much energy coming from the fans, and the adrenaline was pumping for the entire 90 minutes. But it was just an amazing, amazing game, and I thought I had the first goal there, but I was just offside, unfortunately.

Obviously, people refer to me as Zus, or Zusi. I was just very rarely Graham. So the whole "ZUS!" reaction from the crowd, I love it. It's always been something that I've been fond of. But there have been multiple players, usually foreigners who have come to the team, and they'll ask, "Zus, why does the crowd hate you? They always boo you." I start laughing, every single time I'm like, "Nah man, they're saying 'Zus!,' not booing me." Well to be fair, I hope they're saying Zus and not booing.

The Open Cup Final against Seattle in 2012, we had a weather delay that game. We were in the locker room waiting and trying to stay warm and wondering if the fans would stick around, because, I mean, it was the middle of the week. I think we all expected the stadium to be a little less energized and a lot less crowded. And we came out after that weather delay and not a soul had left. They were just as loud, if not louder, when we were walking out again. And it was just like we knew we had it. I know the game went to nearly midnight, but at that point we knew that we had to win that game.

At Children's Mercy Park, there's just been so many moments, whether it's hoisting the Open Cup, one of the many that we've been able to do, or MLS Cup, and we're really lucky that we got to experience those at home. When you're looking back, you remember the results and who you played against, but what you truly remember is the atmosphere that was created in those moments.

I hope that they all know how much they've meant to me throughout my career, and I hope that I've shown the appreciation and hope that they feel the appreciation that I've had for them since day one.

2012 U.S. Open Cup
2013 MLS Cup
2015 U.S. Open Cup
2017 U.S. Open Cup

Graham Zusi is a seven-time MLS All-Star and was an MLS Best XI selection in 2012 and 2013. A 2012 MLS Most Valuable Player finalist, Zusi earned 55 caps for the United States Men's National Team and recorded two assists at the 2014 FIFA World Cup.

Hometown hero Matt Besler lifted his second Lamar Hunt U.S. Open Cup trophy as captain in 2017.

LAMAR'S CUP

A TROPHY THAT MEANS MORE IN KC

For more than a century in the United States, soccer's national champion has been crowned through the U.S. Open Cup, originally known as the National Challenge Cup, and renamed again in 1999 as the Lamar Hunt U.S. Open Cup. It is a competition that Kansas City's MLS entry has excelled at, winning four trophies (only three clubs in the history of the single-elimination competition have won more). With the competition named after the club's founder and American sports pioneer Lamar Hunt, victory in the U.S. Open Cup carries a special meaning for the club. Since the Brooklyn Field Club won the first competition in 1914, the American soccer landscape has evolved, and over the years, 105 more champions from 16 different states and the District of Columbia have been crowned.

Josh Wolff and the 2004 Wizards celebrated the club's first U.S. Open Cup championship at Arrowhead.

2004

In the Wizards' ninth season, they began their journey to the club's first Open Cup title in Georgia with a road game against the Atlanta Silverbacks of the United Soccer League's A-League. Davy Arnaud, thrust into the starting lineup after injuries to Preki and Igor Simutenkov, scored a pair of goals and then assisted on Francisco Gomez's tally two minutes later. Diego Gutierrez put the game away with a goal in the 81st minute as the Wizards advanced by a score of 4-1.

For the quarterfinal, the Wizards returned to the Blue Valley District Activities Complex in Overland Park for the first time since 2001. There they hosted the Dallas Burn in a battle of two MLS teams owned and operated by Hunt. Kansas City cruised to a 4-0 win with four different Wizards scoring in the second half that day: U.S. international Chris Klein, Davy Arnaud, Alex Zotica and rookie Justin Detter. Tony Meola made seven saves to earn his fifth career Open Cup shutout.

More than 2,000 fans (near capacity for the small venue) made the trip on a Tuesday night to Overland Park for the Wizards' semifinal match against the San Jose Earthquakes. Backup Bo Oshoniyi only had to make two saves to earn the clean sheet in a 1-0 win.

Simutenkov was the hero for the Wizards, scoring a penalty kick in first-half stoppage time after Josh Wolff was taken down in the box.

After getting past the Earthquakes, the Wizards hosted the U.S. Open Cup Final at Arrowhead Stadium against the Chicago Fire, a team that had won three U.S. Open Cup titles in their first six years of existence (1998, 2000, 2003). It was a rematch of the 2000 MLS Cup Final that earned the Wizards a 1-0 win and the club's first major trophy.

When the starting lineups were announced, Meola's name was there, despite his injury, but he would admit that he was "really hurting" during the game. On the day, the Wizards' defense was formidable, and Meola had to make only one save against the Fire, but at the same time, Kansas City offense wasn't able to get on the scoresheet either as both teams played 90 minutes without a goal.

Five minutes into extra time, after Wolff was fouled just outside the area, Simutenkov finally broke the deadlock, directing the resulting free kick around the wall and past Fire goalkeeper Henry Ring.

"There was a little more on the line since it was a team that Lamar Hunt was associated with," Meola said of the Wizards' push toward the Cup in 2004. "I don't know if it was so much of an overall club initiative, but I know that [Wizards head coach] Bob Gansler said 'Hey, we've really got to take pride in this tournament,' and everybody bought in because it was an opportunity to put a trophy in the case."

2012

Sporting KC's 2012 U.S. Open Cup run began in the Third Round, where they narrowly avoided an upset. Orlando City SC, who would move on to win the USL Pro (Division 3) regular season championship, gave them all they could handle, but Soony Saad's two second-half goals broke a 1-1 tie and propelled KC to a 3-2 win.

After avoiding an upset in their opening game, Sporting KC's 2012 U.S. Open Cup run was aided by a stout defense. Goalkeeper Jimmy Nielsen led a defense that earned three straight shutouts to advance to the deciding game. They blanked the Colorado Rapids 2-0 thanks to an own goal and a late tally by Teal Bunbury, then they ended the USL Pro Dayton Dutch Lions' Cinderella story in the quarterfinal, 3-0, on the strength of a brace by CJ Sapong. In the Semifinals, Graham Zusi had a goal and an assist in a 2-0 road win over the Philadelphia Union.

In the Final, Sporting faced the Seattle Sounders, trying to become the first team in tournament history to win four straight titles.

At Sporting Park, nearly 19,000 fans waited through a 45-minute lightning delay before kickoff. It was a relatively quiet game until a handball in the box led to a Kei Kamara penalty kick goal in the 84th minute. The KC fans were still in a frenzy from the Kamara goal when Zach Scott, who committed the handball that led to the first goal, redeemed himself by heading home an equalizer for Seattle two minutes later.

The match was the first U.S. Open Cup championship game to go to extra time since the Wizards won it all in 2004. After a tense, scoreless 30 minutes, the stalemate went to a penalty kick shootout.

The tense drama came down to the final kicks. Paulo Nagamura had his attempt in the fifth round saved by Michael Gspurning, but the referee ordered a retake after he ruled the Seattle goalkeeper jumped off his line early. Nagamura made good on the retake to put KC up 3-2, and when Seattle's Eddie Johnson sent his shot well over the crossbar, it gave Sporting their second Open Cup title and prompted a raucous celebration at Sporting Park.

Jimmy Nielsen's penalty kick heroics (and theatrics) led the club to their second Lamar Hunt U.S. Open Cup title.

2015

Three years later, Sporting opened the tournament in Round 4 with the club's first Battle of I-70 when they hosted Saint Louis FC of the USL. Graham Zusi scored the game's lone goal in the 70th minute in what was the first of four straight home games for Kansas City during their Open Cup run.

It was an easier game in the Round of 16 as Sporting crushed FC Dallas, 6-2, behind Dom Dwyer's four-goal performance. Dwyer became the first Sporting KC player to score three or more goals in an Open Cup game.

In the quarterfinal against the Houston Dynamo, Dom Dwyer scored the go-ahead goal on an assist by Krisztian Nemeth in the 86th minute. Then, two minutes later, Dwyer assisted on Nemeth's goal that put the game away, 3-1.

Sporting used the same formula in a 3-1 Semifinal win over Real Salt Lake. After trading goals in the first half, Benny Feilhaber and Nemeth each scored in the final 10 minutes to send them back to the Final.

After four straight home games, KC's luck with hosting games (determined by random draw) ran out as they had to take on the Philadelphia Union at their home stadium in Chester, Pennsylvania. After the Union went into the halftime break up 1-0, Nemeth, who would eventually be named Player of the Tournament, tied the game after receiving a ball on the left wing. The Hungarian then curved it just inside the far post for his tournament-leading fifth goal in the 65th minute.

For the third time in as many championship game appearances, Sporting KC would decide the Final in extra time. After a scoreless 30 minutes of extra time, it came down to penalty kicks. In the eighth round, Tim Melia saved Andrew Wenger's attempt, which set up Jordi Quintilla's carefully placed goal to clinch Sporting a third title, 7-6 on penalties.

2017

Sporting's most recent U.S. Open Cup title came in 2017 and may have been their toughest road to lift the trophy. Kansas City's run to the championship saw them become the first club to defeat five MLS teams en route to an Open Cup title.

SKC began the tournament with three straight shutouts, starting with a 4-0 home win over MLS expansion side Minnesota United, followed by Ike Opara and Gerso Fernandes scoring in a 2-0 road win over the Houston Dynamo.

In the quarterfinal, Sporting's run appeared to be in jeopardy after Seth Sinovic was sent off in the 15th minute. Sporting held on with 10 men, keeping the game scoreless throughout regulation. In extra time, Kansas City's offense exploded shortly after Dallas' Maxi Urruti was sent off with a second yellow card. That evened the match at 10 players each, and KC took advantage about five minutes later as Latif Blessing scored in first-half stoppage time of extra time.

Moments later, Javier Morales of Dallas was shown

Kansas City native Matt Besler lifted his first trophy as captain when Sporting bested the Philadelphia Union on penalty kicks in the 2015 USOC Final.

a straight red card after pulling down Benny Feilhaber on a breakaway opportunity. With the man advantage, Blessing soon doubled the lead. Daniel Salloi put a cherry on top with a goal in the 118th minute to make it 3-0.

It was an inspired performance as the Sporting KC family was grieving the death of co-owner Neal Patterson, who had passed two days earlier at the age of 67.

"If it wasn't for [Neal Patterson] and the rest of the owners, and obviously him being a huge part of keeping this team here, for a lot of us, who knows if we have jobs," said Sporting KC head coach Peter Vermes after the game. "But his commitment to everything about the club was tremendous. What's interesting, and I told the guys this, Neal really thought a lot about this tournament. He thought the U.S. Open Cup was a great tournament … So we talked about that if you can reach down deep, and hopefully that's something that you can reach down for, is that we find a way to win for him."

The drama didn't stop there as the San Jose Earthquakes took Sporting KC to the brink in the semifinals at Children's Mercy Park. After Diego Rubio answered an early San Jose goal, the match would end up being decided from the penalty spot. The shootout lasted six rounds with the deciding goal scored by Matt Besler, followed by Tim Melia's save on Victor Bernardez's attempt. It was the fourth career PK shootout win by Melia (three of them coming with KC).

A sold-out crowd turned out at Children's Mercy Park for the Final where Sporting Kansas City jumped out to an early lead on the New York Red Bulls. The 5-foot-5 Latif Blessing headed home a cross from Graham Zusi to open the scoring in the 25th minute. In the 66th minute, second-half sub Daniel Salloi received a long pass from Benny Feilhaber and touched it past onrushing goalkeeper Ryan Meara to put Kansas City up 2-0. Bradley Wright-Phillips would spoil the clean sheet in second-half stoppage time, but Sporting held on to become just the eighth club in history to win four U.S. Open Cup titles.

"Obviously Lamar [Hunt] was the first owner here in Kansas City. I had the pleasure of playing for him. Great man and an incredible supporter of the game and this league, one of the founders," said Vermes. "So the fact that we bring that [trophy] home has a special place in our club, based on having his name on there, no doubt." ♦

Above, left: The 2017 Open Cup run had extra meaning after the passing of owner Neal Patterson a few days before the Quarterfinal match. Above, right: For the first time in club history, Sporting lifted the Open Cup trophy without needing extra time and/or penalty kicks.

SPORTING

MY STORY: TIM MELIA

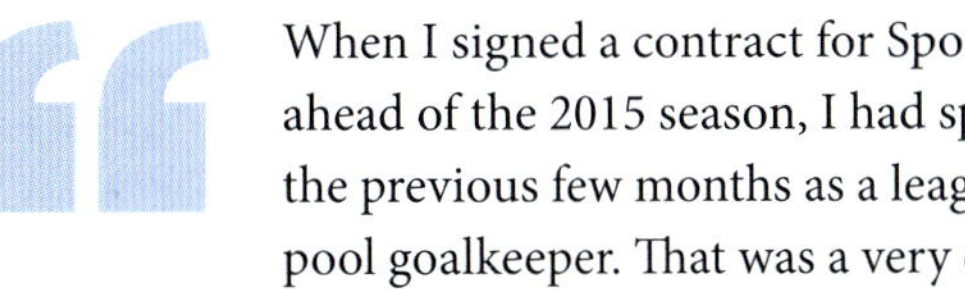

When I signed a contract for Sporting ahead of the 2015 season, I had spent the previous few months as a league pool goalkeeper. That was a very difficult learning experience, but this was a great opportunity to come to an established club. Because I had moved from one club to another, I looked at KC as my last stop.

I was excited to join a club that already had a strong, winning culture in place. It also had an excellent fanbase as well as a great stadium and training facility. The team was also very competitive, having won MLS Cup in 2013. So I entered the 2015 with the mentality of, "All right, I am going to do everything possible to be as prepared as I can. This is my last move as a pro soccer player. If it doesn't work out, I have to assess the reality of the situation and take the next step in my life."

I knew Sporting had a phenomenal fan base and stadium, and that we would probably have a good team. Outside of that, I knew nothing about the city and didn't know what to expect. As someone from New York, I was unfamiliar with the Midwest. In my mind, I thought of cows and green, country acreage everywhere. When I arrived, I was pleasantly surprised to see so much more. As my wife and I have raised our family here, you come to realize that it's a very close-knit, family-oriented city. That's something we've really enjoyed.

At the end of preseason training in 2015, I tried to be optimistic in thinking I would get a shot to play at some point. In early May, eight or nine games into the season, that opportunity came. Our season wasn't going poorly at the time, but we weren't quite where we wanted to be. We made a goalkeeping switch on May 3 for our home game against the Chicago Fire.

The first thing I remember about that game is running way off my line and heading the ball. I will never forget that moment for the rest of my life. It was like eight years of anxiety had just come out in one thumping header. I'm glad I made that play, and I'm glad I've been able to play regularly for this club ever since.

The 2017 U.S. Open Cup Final against the New York Red Bulls at Children's Mercy Park was the loudest game I've ever played in. The environment throughout that game—the energy and the noise in the jam-packed stadium, and winning 2-1 and painting the wall—that's something that sticks with you forever.

When you get the opportunity to walk through the tunnel at Children's Mercy Park and play in this electric environment, you get a true feel for the culture the fans have built. They are here to support us through the good and the bad. We've had some great years and some less successful years, and the fans are just as supportive—if not more supportive—when times are tough. You don't see that many places. That is the culture of the city and the region. The supporter culture here is priceless, and these are the types of places you want to be as an athlete.

I love the occasions when I'm able to chat and have normal conversations with fans. I'll see them out at dinner, and someone will come up to me and just start talking and expressing their appreciation. That's the culture and the environment that Kansas City has built. People rally around their hometown teams, businesses, restaurants and landmarks.

If I'm being totally honest, it was never my plan to wind up in Kansas City. When I left college, I was determined to stay in New York and try to attach to a New York team. But your master plan doesn't always work. In the end, I couldn't be happier that I found such a special club, community, neighborhood and place to raise my children. Regardless of what happens in the future, Kansas City is a place that I will always cherish.

2015 U.S. Open Cup
2017 U.S. Open Cup

Tim Melia was named MLS Comeback Player of the Year in 2015 and went on to earn MLS Goalkeeper of the Year and MLS Best XI honors in 2017. Melia was also recognized as the team's Most Valuable Player in 2017, followed by team Defensive Player of the Year accolades in 2018 and 2019.

MY STORY: PETER VERMES

AS PLAYER

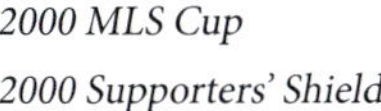

2000 MLS Cup
2000 Supporters' Shield

AS COACH

2012 U.S. Open Cup
2013 MLS Cup
2015 U.S. Open Cup
2017 U.S. Open Cup

Peter Vermes was inducted into the National Soccer Hall of Fame in 2013 after earning 66 caps with the U.S. Men's National Team. Vermes represented the United States at the 1988 Summer Olympics and 1990 FIFA World Cup. In KC, Vermes was named MLS Defender of the Year and MLS Best XI selection in 2000. A three-time finalist for MLS Coach of the Year, Vermes has led Sporting to four first-place finishes since becoming head coach in 2009. In 2019, he received the league's inaugural MLS Sporting Executive of the Year award.

"I never would have thought that I was ever going to play in Kansas City. Let's put it that way. And I knew that they were trying to trade for me.

My wife and I are both from New Jersey. So our plan was, when I'm done playing, we're going to move back to New Jersey because all of our family was there. I came here in January of 2000. She came in about June, because she stayed while the kids finished school and we sold the house. And so she had only spent maybe five or six months here when we went home for Christmas. We drove home for Christmas and on the way back to KC, she said, "I would never want to move back to New Jersey, and I really like living in Kansas City." And so that was an interesting transformation.

In '96, I played for New York. And in that year, we went to the conference final. The Colorado Rapids were the worst team in the league, and I was traded to them for the next season, and we went to the [MLS Cup] final that year. Three years later, I was traded to Kansas City, and they were the worst team in the league. I already had some experience with going into a team that wasn't very good. And then we went to the final and we won.

Brian Bliss had gotten a job as an assistant with Bob Gansler, and Brian and I played together and for Gans' [on the U.S. National Team in 1990]. So Brian reached out to me asked if I would come to KC if they traded for me. "Absolutely." Because at that point it was only about soccer for me. Obviously, I wanted my family to have a good place to live. But for me, the decision was always based on soccer. I was up for the opportunity to play for Bob Gansler again.

What's interesting about the 2000 team is how it was able to come together. Bob changed a boatload of players. He didn't change two or three players or add two or three players—he friggin' wiped the team out. Changed at least half, if not more, of the personnel. So it's almost like an expansion team, because you're starting from scratch. It was by far the most mentally tough team that I played on. It was a team that was full of strong personalities. Winners. In really tough moments, we knew how to get the job done.

From an individual perspective, the Defender of the Year award is probably the most meaningful one of my career, along with the MLS Best XI. Because my entire childhood and first eight years of my career, I played as a center forward. They're the antithesis of each other, right? It means so much, because I never considered myself to be this great player. I thought I was a good player. It was a really proud moment, because I was able to prove that I was a "soccer player," not just a specialist.

I always thought I was very lucky and fortunate to be doing what I was doing [playing soccer.] It's part of my personality. I always felt a responsibility to the fans and the ownership groups—because if they didn't feel like this was something they had passion for, none of us would have jobs to be able to do what we love to do. So I never forgot that.

One story as a player that I'll never forget: I remember training the day before the 2000 Final, Lamar Hunt showed up with Clark and said "Hey, listen, I haven't won a championship since the start of the 1970s." So, you get taken aback when you hear that, and it's Lamar Hunt talking to you. And at the celebration party afterwards, he was happy as could be, you know? And I think it was great that we were able to repay him.

I knew what I wanted to do. My goal age was 35, and I played until I was 36. I had this goal that when I retired I wanted to be in a position where I could make the decision for my next profession. It was going to be based on what I wanted to do, not what I had to do. My wife and I worked really hard to make that happen. It took me about six months to decide, because I had all these different offers and opportunities that were out there. So I took over a youth club in the Overland Park area called the Blue Valley Soccer Club.

That experience was priceless, because, to be honest with you, there's a lot of similarities between a youth soccer club and a professional soccer club. I gained a tremendous amount of experience doing that job. At the same time, I was also the assistant for the U20 Men's National Team and went to the FIFA Youth World Championship in 2005 with Sigi Schmid, as one of his assistants. I sat on the board of directors for U.S. Soccer for just about two decades. I was a chairman of the Athletes Council. I was the athlete representative for the Olympic Games. I sat on the U.S. Soccer Foundation; I was doing a lot of stuff within soccer at the time.

In youth sports, I got to know a lot more of the community than when I was a professional player. Because I was around parents and their children, the connections I was making were ... multiply it by a thousand compared to when I was a player. I was coming across a lot of people in the city.

My first introduction to the club was Robb Heineman. We got introduced and then pretty quickly, they hired me as a consultant. At first I thought they were just building a stadium. Then I found out they're possibly going to buy the team. It was like I was in a Formula One car. And the first day I got to see it and the next day he said, drive it. It was that fast.

I felt I had a really good idea of what a Sporting Director should do and what the responsibilities were, and how they can make sure that they built a real club. And that was really what I was excited about the most—building a club. Getting that opportunity, I appreciated the trust that was put in me. And I also understood the responsibility. Probably more so than anyone else did, because I thought of it as my only opportunity.

I've been with the ownership group since the beginning, and what I think is amazing is their evolution. Their involvement, their understanding and their leadership is incredible ... they took a business opportunity and just completely transformed it. And now they're leaders in the sports and soccer industry in this country. It says so much about who they are and why they're successful.

It means a lot to me, having played here and now coaching here. I've been offered other opportunities to go and do other things. I think a lot of people have said, "Oh, why wouldn't you do that?" "You should go and do that," for all these different reasons. Blah blah blah. But the fact of the matter is, I've always believed in the project here, and I always wanted to be a part of building that project.

On game day, I definitely have my routine. It's not superstition, it's just routine, and it's really strange. Driving to Children's Mercy Park or the Compass Minerals Performance National Performance Center is the same route. On game days, I come a different way. I don't know why that is, and I don't know how it started.

Another that I don't think most people know or don't pay attention to: I don't come out for warm ups. There are double doors that lead from the hallway to the field entrance and if I stand there, I can hear the national anthem. I stand at attention and have my hand on my heart. But I always come out right after that, because, to be honest with you, I'm so jazzed up for the game. So excited for it. It's what I did in the first game when the place opened up in 2011, and I've done it ever since.

There's no better feeling for me than when the national anthem is done and I come out and go over to welcome the other staff to Children's Mercy Park. The second I walk through that set of doors I always get goosebumps and a little bit of the hair stands up on my neck because of that ambience and that electricity in the stadium from the fans. The fans are what make the game.

SPORTING KC KIT HISTORY
2011- PRESENT

Light blue and navy have been a staple sartorial combination for centuries. Sporting's kit options from any given season—or across many years combined—may look different, but when taken together as a whole, they always feel like a cohesive collection.

Whether it's Sporting Blue or Dark Indigo; hoops, argyle or state line, the club's jerseys have always been designed to satisfy one requirement: They must look as good off the field as they do on it.

2011-12

2011-13

2013-14

2013-14

2014-15

2015-16

2015-16

2016-17

2017-18

2018-19

2019-20

2020-21

2021-22

Some things never go out of style. Building on the heritage and culture of an iconic design both for Sporting Kansas City and the global sport, Sporting's 2021 primary kit is an evolution of one of the most popular looks in Club history. Hoops 3.0 represents both Sporting's past and its future.

The kit also features The Victory Project, a part of the club's "Force For Good" campaign. Throughout the 2021 season, the Victory Project will tell the story of and lift other local organizations meeting the needs of the Kansas City community in challenging times.

2011-2020

SPORTING

A KANSAS CITY SOCCER TIMELINE

11.08.11
Sporting KC striker C.J. Sapong named 2011 MLS Rookie of the Year

12.20.11
Graham Zusi named MLS Breakout Player of the Year

05.30.12
Tony Meola inducted into National Soccer Hall of Fame

08.08.12
Sporting Kansas City wins Lamar Hunt U.S. Open Cup in penalty kick shootout over Seattle Sounders FC

11.20.12
Matt Besler named MLS Defender of the Year

11.28.12
Jimmy Nielsen named 2012 MLS Allstate Goalkeeper of the Year

11.17.10
Sporting Kansas City unveiled as club's new identity

2010

2011

03.23.11
Chad Ochocinco begins tryout with Sporting Kansas City

06.04.11
Bob Gansler inducted into National Soccer Hall of Fame

06.09.11
Livestrong Sporting Park inaugural match, SKC vs. CHI

08.17.11
Jimmy Nielsen hit in head by Omar Bravo bobblehead

08.17.11
Brisket Bob makes his debut

11.06.11
Then-record crowd of 20,839 attends Eastern Conference Championship

2013

01.17.13
Sporting Kansas City announces Ivy Funds as the club's first-ever jersey sponsor

VICTORY
PROJECT
A FOUNDATION OF SPORTING KC

04.05.13
Sporting KC launches The Victory Project

07.31.13
Sporting Park hosts the 2013 AT&T MLS All-Star Game

10.11.13
Peter Vermes inducted into National Soccer Hall of Fame

12.07.13
Sporting Kansas City wins 2013 MLS Cup, defeating Real Salt Lake 7-6 on penalty kicks after a 1-1 draw

07.19.14
Sporting Kansas City signs Matt Besler and Graham Zusi to long-term Designated Player contracts through 2018

09.30.15
Sporting Kansas City wins the 2015 Lamar Hunt U.S. Open Cup, defeating the Philadelphia Union 7-6 on penalty kicks after a 1-1 draw

10.22.15
Sporting Club launches Swope Park Rangers as USL expands to Kansas City

11.18.15
Goalkeeper Tim Melia is named the MLS Comeback Player of the Year in his first season with Sporting KC

12.03.15
Krisztian Nemeth wins the 2015 AT&T Goal of the Year for his stunning solo run and finish against the Portland Timbers on Oct. 3

07.29.17
Victory Project honoree chair changed to orange, in honor of Neal Patterson's favorite color

09.20.17
Sporting KC crowned Lamar Hunt U.S. Open Cup champions with 2-1 win over New York Red Bulls at Children's Mercy Park

11.09.17
Ike Opara named MLS Defender of the Year

11.16.17
Tim Melia named MLS Goalkeeper of the Year

03.15.18
Kansas City included as Candidate Host City in United Bid to host the 2026 FIFA World Cup

01.25.16
Jake Reid, an executive at the club since 2010, named Sporting Kansas City President; Reid later becomes President and CEO on April 18, 2018

03.26.16
Swope Park Rangers, now known as Sporting KC II, play inaugural USL match at Children's Mercy Park

07.09.17
Sporting Club co-owner Neal Patterson dies at age 67 after battle with cancer

02.24.16
No Other Pub opens in the Kansas City Power & Light District through a partnership between Sporting Kansas City, The Cordish Companies and Entertainment Consulting International

07.10.16
Ceremonial groundbreaking held for Pinnacle

06.09.18
Matt Besler surpasses Davy Arnaud for most MLS regu-lar-season appearances in club history, playing his 241st game against the Portland Timbers

03.12.20
Major League Soccer suspends the 2020 regular season due to the COVID-19 pandemic

11.22.20
Tim Melia makes MLS history as the first keeper to save all three penalties in a shootout

05.16.18
Pinnacle National Development Center grand opening

12.10.19
Sporting acquires Mexican striker Alan Pulido on a club-record transfer fee from Liga MX powerhouse Chivas de Guadalajara

07.12.20
Sporting returns to play in the MLS is Back Tournament, facing Minnesota United FC after a four-month hiatus in MLS action

2011 - PRESENT

THE EXP

ERIENCE

Around this team and around this stadium, people say "We." This club has become part of the community, an integral part of the modern Kansas City. At Children's Mercy Park, those in the crowd are more than fans, louder than supporters and bigger than themselves. It is a place where we raise our voices in unison, fly our colors with pride and embrace our own traditions. We come together for city and club. We sway when we win.
A quarter century in the making, this is the Sporting Experience.

NO OTHER CLUB

A SUPPORTERS' ORAL HISTORY

On June 6, 1995, it was announced that Kansas City would have its own Major League Soccer team. The team's identity, nickname and team colors would be built from scratch. But sports loyalty is an organic thing and while the Wiz would play a full schedule in 1996, they made very little impact on the larger Kansas City sports scene, still preoccupied at the time with recovering from the gutshot home playoff loss that ended the Chiefs' 1995 season and the Royals' indifferent 70-74 record in the year after baseball's strike canceled the World Series.

From the earliest stages, though, a diehard coterie of fans began gravitating to the games. Soon enough, they found one another and became intent on building a supporter culture that would become integral to the Kansas City soccer experience.

The Cauldron celebrated both eras of the club's heritage, Wizards and Sporting, to mark the 20th anniversary in 2016.

so many people want to say hi, chat and take photos with Brisket Bob. And even after almost 10 years, I still get quite a few people on match day who are confused and either think I'm selling BBQ, or they just have no idea what the schtick is and I have to explain to them, "Well, in Portland, they have this guy named Timber Joey …" However, it is a lot of fun to meet so many new people. I am the Kansas City soccer community's premier D-list celebrity.

TIFO TIME

Have you ever wondered about the giant banners that are hung from the bridge over the Supporters' Stand before matches? Here are the histories of a few of the more famous ones. Note: "Tifo" is a term for these banners that comes from the Italian word "tifosi," which basically means "supporters clubs," but because Italian clubs led the way in this kind of fan culture, that's the way it's used in English now.

ADAM YARNEVICH: I have only designed two tifos/banners over the years, the "Night King" and the "HOME OF THE BRAVE" banner we hang during U.S. national team matches, and I've mostly stuck to merch design like scarves and T-shirts. After that particular episode of "Game of Thrones" aired, I thought, "That would be a great tifo, but it would have to be rigged." It struck me as one of the better "Come at me, bro" moments in recent pop-culture history, so I dug that aspect of it. I did a quick, paint by numbers illustration of the design in Illustrator and showed the rest of the Cauldron board. Everyone liked it, so Tifo Team Six went to work figuring out the logistics and getting it produced. Mark, Dan, Eli and all of those guys planned it all out: A painting schedule, how to rig it and even added to it by making the "Welcome to the Blue Hell" banner be in the "GOT" typeface for that particular presentation. I remember us all being relieved that no one else had done the exact same "GOT" design.

The actual construction and painting of a tifo goes into production many weeks before its unveiling, and you are always just hoping some other supporters' group doesn't come up with something similar during that time.

ELI SPENCER (Tifo team): Making the tifos is a huge community effort that's way bigger than the tifo team. It takes everybody in the Cauldron coming out. We'll have a big painting day; we'll call

The Night King made his one and only appearance in Kansas City on May 1, 2016.

everybody out. It's paint by numbers. So … people should really come help us paint.

ADAM YARNEVICH: The biggest thing I think that caught everyone off guard was the response to it. There were a lot of soccer news outlets around the world that wrote about it, and the comments were overwhelmingly positive. It was really cool that some soccer publication in Belgium (or wherever it was) was writing about the Cauldron.

ELI SPENCER: It got A LOT of attention. It was really funny because we're waiting as the anthem is going on, and the players are getting pumped up for the game, but they've done it a million times. But WE'RE sitting there and I felt like I was getting ready to go into a game. What if I pull this thing and my hand slips? What if it breaks and comes tumbling down? So it was nerve-wracking and then we did it. And seeing people's reaction was … The Best.

ADAM YARNEVICH: We had many people ask when they would see the Night King tifo again, and we always had to tell them that they only go up once. The average giant tifo's lifespan is about 45 seconds. People are amazed that a group of people would put that much time and effort into something that is only seen for a minute. But that's what supporters do. Well, the crazy ones.

SAM PIERRON: The phrase "Welcome To The Blue Hell" comes from a banner that Matt Spoonmore made in the CAB era.

MATT SPOONMORE: I still have the banner. At Fenerbahce in Turkey, they used to have this banner that they put up when Man U played there that said, "Welcome To Hell." I took that and added "Your Blue" in German, because they had great banners.

SAM PIERRON: The German was wrong, but whatever. That's the fault of the German woman who did the translation, ironically.

MATT SPOONMORE: Yeah, it says "Welcome To Her Blue Hell."

SAM PIERRON: Maybe it's commentary.

AN EXTENDED FAMILY

Though the name of the new stadium changed from Livestrong Park to Sporting Park, and finally Children's Mercy Park, the Cauldron remained the same, located in the north stand, the ever-present Blue Hell for opponents. And as the club has grown, so has the organized supporters culture, beyond the groups that congregate in the Supporters' Stand to include other parts of the stadium as well as groups that just focus on community activities.

SAM PIERRON: Any discussion of Sporting supporters is lacking if you don't talk about the late Barb Goebel and the Ladies of SKC. They're part of the Cauldron ISC and are one of the best venues for fans from all around the stadium to get together outside of the games.

MATT KILLINGSWORTH (Former South Stand SC President): As we got to fall in the 2011 season, we reached out to Sean Dane and Sam Pierron about creating something in the south end to complement the Cauldron. Because of the open South Stand seating, and all the groups that were sold there, we knew it would need to be family friendly. Many of our founders were new to the sport or to SKC, and our core desire was to share the game with friends. Over time the South Stand SC became a group of friends to which others were drawn.

BAHIA BROWN (Former South Stand SC President): We have seven

Barb Goebel was a dedicated long-time Sporting fan who sadly passed away in 2020.

What began with a small group of diehard Wizards fans behind the goal at Arrowhead has grown into a community, a family and a "Cauldron City."

affiliate groups based all around, including Omaha, the Pacific Northwest, the Rockies, even Gladstone!

DEREK GATHRIGHT (Long-time supporter and Heart of America Soccer Foundation founder): We never envisioned that our stadium would be one of the premier places in the world to watch a game of soccer. All of that would seem greater than a dream come true. A fantasy. We just wanted to keep watching soccer in our hometown.

SAM PIERRON: We're now 10 seasons into playing at Sporting Park, so it's sometimes easy to forget just how amazing it is and the sea change it represented in KC soccer supporters' culture. As much as I don't want to be the hipster saying you had to be there during the early days to appreciate it; the fact is that it is uniquely rewarding to have seen it all happen and to wind up in this incredible place. The final few sentences in Jhumpa Lahiri's excellent collection of short stories, Interpreter of Maladies, are, I think, apropos: "Still, there are times I am bewildered by each mile I have traveled, each meal I have eaten, each person I have known, each room in which I have slept. As ordinary as it all appears, there are times when it is beyond my imagination."

JOSUE MOLINA (Current Cauldron President): I played soccer all through middle school and played on my high school J.V. team until I wrecked my knee. And I was like, you know what, I really like playing the tuba and trombone … I'm going to focus on that for a while. But my father (from Honduras) took me to games from 1996 through high school. We went to four or five games a year religiously, trying to just be out there and having a good time. The way that I got into international soccer was watching Honduras on pay per view or some obscure channel or going to someone's house with a movable satellite dish and watching Honduras play that way, but I was always 100 percent behind the U.S.

I'm an introverted person. I sometimes dread being in the middle leading chants and playing the trombone. I'll be on the drive out to the game, and I'll just be like, I don't really want to do this again. And then once I'm in the parking lot, everything changes. I remember the first time I was in the Cauldron. It was at Blue Valley Some Direction. Hector posted on Facebook asking if anyone played an instrument, so I brought my trombone. Jeff Szajnuk said it would be a good idea if we all met up at the Blue Moose before the game and then walked over. It was cold and rainy, and it was a long walk.

I'm not a very religious person, but going to soccer games is church for me, because regardless of how the game plays out, I'm going to go home with a smile on my face. I drink a lot of beer, hang out with people who I truly, truly care about, leave everything I have in the stands, and chant and be ridiculous and do everything I can.

The Cauldron has become part of my extended family. You know, in my teaching career, I've taught with people for 10 years now, but the Cauldron feels more like home than my school. ♦

LIVE. WORK. BANK
mazuma
ADVOCARE
adidas
adidas
adidas
Ivy

SPORTING HERITAGE

Sports traditions are both a link to the past and a bridge to the future. They are passed from one generation to the next, connecting fervent fans together while weaving the very fabric of the teams they support. Nowhere is this more evident than at Children's Mercy Park, where Sporting Kansas City and its supporters have redefined what it means to attend a soccer match.

Sporting's move into the world-class stadium in 2011 marked the dawn of a new, tradition-rich era of soccer in Kansas City. Some traditions take place minutes before kickoff, creating an electric atmosphere and setting the stage for Sporting to pursue victory. Others take place after full time, celebrating victories and bonding players to the passionate fans who sing and cheer for all 90 minutes.

As the heart and soul of Sporting, these traditions preserve the club's history and invite all guests at Children's Mercy Park to be part of a special story that evolves from one season to the next.

THE SWAY

Peter Vermes and his captain Matt Besler went to the leadership of the Cauldron with an idea: Together, could they come up with a new tradition for after every win? They were looking for something the fans and players could do together to honor each other—the players for the effort on the field and the fans for the energy in the stands that spurred them on.

It didn't take long for the group to land on an idea. "The Sway" was born.

After every win at home—or even at the MLS is Back Tournament during the 2020 season disrupted by the COVID pandemic—the players make their way to the goal box in front of the Cauldron, lock arms around each other, and sway as they sing along with the fans.

"Oh when the Wiz go marching in ..."

It starts slow and builds to a raucous drum celebration and is the perfect encapsulation of what makes the Sporting family so special: Togetherness.

AWAY TICKETS & "ROADDRON"

During development of the stadium and the transition to Sporting, the club asked fans what kind of things they wanted for being season ticket members. "Free tickets to road games" was one of the responses, and an idea that started as a half-joking suggestion on an internet message board has grown into one of the most unique fan benefits in all of sports.

Since 2011, Sporting has covered the cost of tickets for any traveling season ticket members in what has become affectionately known as the "Roaddron." Open to all, Cauldron and non-Cauldron fans alike, the Roaddron has seen groups of 1,000+ travel to watch their club play all over the United States, and even Champions League matches in Mexico.

The Roaddron has become famous throughout MLS, and Sporting supporters are now known as one of the best traveling fanbases in all of American sports.

VICTORY PROJECT HONOREE

On April 5, 2013, The Victory Project hosted its first honoree, Xander Reynolds, in the Victory Suite at Sporting Park. Xander has a brain tumor that has caused blindness in one eye and severely diminished vision in the other. The 8-year-old was the guest of honor at the match, which also marked the official launch of the foundation.

Less than a month after being honored—thanks to donations from Sporting KC fans—Xander's mother was able to use the money raised to purchase the reading device he needed to complete classwork at home.

So far, the Victory Project has welcomed nearly 150 children, along with their friends and families as special VIP guests. The all-access experience includes a chance to attend a training session and a behind-the-scenes tour of the stadium before being honored on the videoboard and by the Cauldron leading the entire stadium in chanting their name.

I BELIEVE THAT WE WILL WIN

I
I believe
I believe that
I believe that we
I believe that we will win!

Before the whistle even blows, the visitors know they're not just going up against the 11 blue-clad opponents on the pitch, they're taking on 18,500+ more in the stands.

It caught fire in 2011 after the KC chapter of American Outlaws introduced it during the June 14 USA vs. Guadalupe match at Livestrong Sporting Park during that summer's Gold Cup, and it has since become synonymous with Sporting KC.

Today, big matches are marked with a guest chant-leader, which has included mayors, TVP honorees, Sporting Legends, iconic KC rapper Tech N9ne, and NFL MVP Patrick Mahomes and the Kansas City Chiefs.

PAINT THE WALL

It began with a simple post on social media from co-owner Robb Heineman in the lead up to the 2012 season that became a rallying cry for Sporting fans everywhere: #PaintTheWall

The wall in the northwest corner of Children's Mercy Park represents Sporting's past, its future, and always the ultimate goal: bringing more championships to the greatest fans in Major League Soccer.

There is no higher honor in the club than "Painting the Wall" to acknowledge another trophy raised.

The captain first climbs the ladder to celebrate the victory with spray paint, which is later converted to the silver letterting. The wall also honors one of Sporting's owners, the late Neal Patterson, who passed away during the club's memorable 2017 U.S. Open Cup run.

THE SPORTING EXPERIENCE

A MATCHDAY IN THE LIFE OF CHILDREN'S MERCY PARK

Children's Mercy Park
TOYOTA

BLUE KC SAMARITAN SUITE
SPORT

WELCOME TO THE BLUE HELL
KWIKGOAL
enterprise
SPORTING

45
52
SPORTING
KANSAS CITY

ELCOME TO THE BLUE

14
A-150

DIEGO RUBIO
11
ILIE
6
OPARA
ESCOBAR
29
62
33

K. BANK.
FOR LIFE
makita
5

SALLOI
20
Ivy
INVESTMENTS
SPORTING
KANSAS CITY
COLUMBUS CREW
14
17
29
SeatGeek

adidas
adidas
adidas
adidas

I BELIEVE THAT
WE WILL WIN!

IVY FUNDS

96
WELCOME TO
SPORTING

WELCOME TO

SKC

SPORTING KC
1996

Children's Mercy Park
BUD
LIGHT
OUR SOCCER

FABIAN
10

ADVOCARE
POLSTER
2
66

BESLER
5
COLLIN
78

14
GERSO
7

STEWARD

CLUB
8
15
19
11

SPORTING KANSAS CITY
SKC
SKC
MELIA
29
21
20
6

FEILHABER
30

SUPPORTERS
SHIELD
2000

ORTING
ANSAS CITY
SPORTING
MLS CUP
HAMPIONS
2000
2013
U.S. OPEN CUP
CHAMPIONS
2004
2012
2015
2017
EXIT

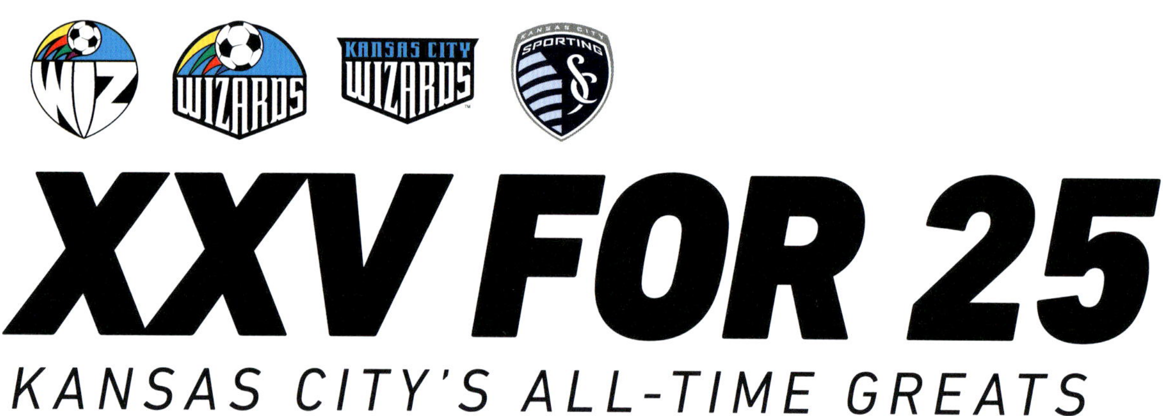

XXV FOR 25

KANSAS CITY'S ALL-TIME GREATS

In 25 seasons, 247 different players have worn the colors of the Kansas City Wiz, the Kansas City Wizards and Sporting Kansas City. Over that time, 45 players have made at least 100 appearances for the club.

But which players have been most exemplary over the history of the club? We asked eight experts to name the club's all-time greatest 25 players.

The voters were: manager and Sporting Legend Peter Vermes; assistant coach and Sporting Legend Kerry Zavagnin; creative director Chad Reynolds; content producer Sam Kovzan; communications director Kurt Austin; chief communications officer Rob Thomson; Mystics/Cauldron founder and former Wizards and Sporting staffer Sam Pierron; "The Final Whistle" post-match show host and former staffer Dave Borchardt.

On the following pages, find the 25 members of the Wiz/Wizards/Sporting 25th Anniversary XXV. While some players played more than one position during their time with the club, they were placed in the position where each had the greatest impact.

GOALKEEPERS

TIM MELIA

2015-PRESENT

TONY MEOLA

1999-2004

JIMMY NIELSEN

2010-2013

DEFENDERS

5

MATT BESLER

2009-2020

78

AURÉLIEN COLLIN

2011-2014

7

CHANCE MYERS

2008-2016

3

IKE OPARA

2013-2018

12

JIMMY CONRAD

2003-2010

3

NICK GARCIA

2000-2007

15

SETH SINOVIC

2011-2019

6

PETER VERMES

2000-2002

MIDFIELDERS

15

ROGER ESPINOZA

2008-2012, 2015-PRESENT

10

BENNY FEILHABER

2013-2017, 2019

17

CHRIS KLEIN

1998-2005

5

KERRY ZAVAGNIN

2000-2008

11

PREKI

1996-2000, 2002-2005

6

PAULO NAGAMURA

2012-2016

8

GRAHAM ZUSI

2009-PRESENT

ATTACKERS

22

DAVY ARNAUD

2002-2011

14

DOM DWYER

2012-2017

7

JOHNNY RUSSELL

2018-PRESENT

12

"DIGITAL" TAKAWIRA

1996-1999

MO JOHNSTON

1996-2001

KEI KAMARA

2009-2013

JOSH WOLFF

2003-2006, 2008-2010

XI CLASSIC WINS

Attempting to select the greatest matches in club history is an enjoyable, if ultimately thankless, task. How does one weigh the significance of a particular moment with the resonance of what sticks in the memory? Is a match that clinches the Supporters Shield inherently more or less important than a loss in an MLS Cup Final?

Do you value flashes of individual brilliance, or the overall magnitude and emotions of a moment? Are you drawn to high-scoring shootouts, like the Wiz' barn-burner 6-4 win over Columbus in 1996? Or lock-down defensive performances like the 2000 MLS Cup?

One of the best criteria is: Can you tell the history of the club without mentioning this given game? On that basis, these eleven matches—all wins—are each an unmissable piece in the rich mosaic history of this club. Each supporter will have his or her own personal list; while the following eleven matches won't end the argument, they are certainly a good place to start to the discussion.

October 6, 2000

1    0

2000 MLS Cup Semifinal Series - Game 3
Arrowhead Stadium

KC Bench: Oshoniyi, Okafor, Brown, Johnson, Jakins, Gomez, Figueroa, Wilson, Dotsenko

Molnar (PK)	⚽ 21'	Vanney	36'
Garcia	40'		
Molnar	50'		
Johnston	58'		
Zavagnin	76'		

MINI-GAME (Golden Goal):

Molnar ⚽ 96'

KC Advances 1–0 in Mini-Game after 4–4 tie on points

October 15, 2000

1    0

MLS Cup 2000
Robert F. Kennedy Memorial Stadium

KC Substitutes:
Okafor for Preki 74'
Gomez for Klein 89'

KC Bench: Oshoniyi, Brown, Figueroa, Byaruhanga, Johnson

Molnar	⚽ 11'	Kovalenko	47'
Johnston	48'	Bonseu	76'
Garcia	58'		
Meola	76'		

September 22, 2004

1    0

2004 U.S. Open Cup Final

Arrowhead Stadium

KC Substitutes:
Simutenkov for Gomez 46'
Graham for Jewsbury 68'

KC Bench: Oshoniyi, Thomas, Walsh, Taylor, Detter

Gutierrez	80'
Simutenkov	95'

Pause	21'

October 30, 2004

3    0

2004 Western Conference Semifinals - Leg 2

Arrowhead Stadium

KC Substitutes:
Simutenkov for Stephenson 69'
Walsh for Zavagnin 86'
Graham for Zotinca 90+4'

KC Bench: Hesmer, Thomas, Gomez, Detter, Taylor

Stephenson	26'
Jewsbury	46'
Ching (OG)	48'
Arnaud	56'
Gutierrez	78'
Jewsbury	90+2'

Donovan	43'

KC Advances 3-2 On Aggregate

July 25, 2010

2   1

International Friendly

Arrowhead Stadium

KC Substitutes:
Besler for Rocastle 44'
Kronberg for Nielsen 46'
Aiyegbusi for Smith 58'
Chhetri for Bunbury 69'
Jewsbury for Arnaud 69'
Zusi for Auvray 78'
Myers for Kamara 83'

KC Bench: Leathers, Hohlbein, Diop, Wolff

Arnaud	11'
Conrad	39'
Kamara	42'
Kamara	43'

Giggs	33'
Berbatov (PK)	41'
Gibson	63'

August 8, 2012

1  

1

2012 U.S. Open Cup Final
Livestrong Sporting Park

GSPURNING
HURTADO SCOTT
IANNI GONZALEZ
ALONSO ROSE
ROSALES CASKEY
MONTERO JOHNSON

KAMARA BUNBURY ZUSI
ESPINOZA NAGAMURA
CESAR
SINOVIC BESLER OLUM MYERS
NIELSEN

SKC Substitutes:
Sapong for Bunbury 89′
Harrington for Sinovic 100′

SKC Bench: Kronberg, Saad, Marković, Peterson, Thomas

Kamara (PK)	⚽ 84′	Alonso	🟨	4′
		Rosales	🟨	57′
		Ianni	🟨	73′
		Scott	⚽	86′
		Scott	🟨	93′
		Ianni	🟨🟥	118′

PENALTY KICKS:

SKC Wins in Penalties (3-2)

November 23, 2013

2 

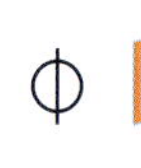 

1

2013 Eastern Conference Finals - Leg 2
Sporting Park

SKC Substitutes:
Opara for Feilhaber 84′
Peterson for Zusi 90′
Bieler for Dwyer 90′

SKC Bench: Kronberg, Saad, Bessone, Bunbury

Sapong	⚽ 14′	Garcia	⚽	3′
Dwyer	⚽ 63′	Garcia	🟨	37′
		Brunner	🟨	85′

SKC Advances 2-1 on Aggregate

December 7, 2013

1 

1

MLS Cup 2013
Sporting Park

SKC Substitutes:
Olum for Rosell 8′
Bieler for Dwyer 72′

SKC Bench: Bunbury, Opara, Kronberg, Peterson, Bessone

Collin	🟨	35′	Wingert	🟨	24′
Collin	⚽	76′	Saborio	🟨	44′
Feilhaber	🟨	103′	Saborio	⚽	52′
			Beckerman	🟨	100′

PENALTY KICKS:

SKC Wins in Penalties (7-6)

September 30, 2015

1    1

2015 U.S. Open Cup Final
PPL Park

BLAKE
EDU, MARQUEZ
GADDIS, FABINHO
BARNETTA, MAIDANA, LAHOUD
NOGUIERA, LE TOUX
SAPONG

DWYER
NEMETH, ZUSI
FEILHABER, MUSTIVAR, NAGAMURA
SINOVIC, MYERS
BESLER, ELLIS
MELIA

SKC Substitutes:
Quintilla for Mustivar 66'
Abdul-Salaam for Sinovic 78'
Peterson for Myers 112'

SKC Bench: Kempin, Palmer-Brown, Anor, Lopez

Lahoud	yellow card	21'
Le Toux	goal	23'
Barnetta	yellow card	58'
Sapong	yellow card	90+1'
Ellis	yellow card	29'
Sinovic	yellow card	34'
Nemeth	goal	65'
Quintilla	yellow card	71'
Besler	yellow card	86'
Nagamura	yellow card	94'
Zusi	yellow card	104'
Myers	yellow card	106'

PENALTY KICKS:

SKC Wins in Penalties (7-6)

July 11, 2017

3    0

2017 U.S. Open Cup Quarterfinal
Children's Mercy Park

SKC Substitutes:
Salloi for Gerso 85'
Feilhaber for Rubio 91'
Ellis for Opara 105+5'

SKC Bench: Dykstra, Storm, Mustivar, Saad

Sinovic	red card	15'
Espinoza	yellow card	45+3'
Medranda	yellow card	65'
Blessing	goal	105+3'
Blessing	goal	105+8'
Salloi	goal	118'
Ulloa	yellow card	45+2'
Diaz	yellow card	62'
Urruti	yellow card	90'
Urruti	yellow card, red card	101'
Morales	red card	105+5'
Harris	yellow card	120'

September 20, 2017

2 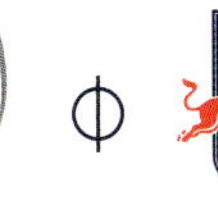  1

2017 U.S. Open Cup Final
Children's Mercy Park

MEARA
ESCOBAR, LONG, LAWRENCE
ADAMS, MURRILO
KLEJSTAN, FELIPE
DAVIS, MUYL
WRIGHT-PHILLIPS

RUBIO
BLESSING, GERSO
FEILHABER, ILIE, ESPINOZA
SINOVIC, ZUSI
BESLER, OPARA
MELIA

SKC Substitutes:
Salloi for Blessing 43'
Medranda for Gerso 56'
Oliveira for Rubio 82'

SKC Bench: Zendejas, Abdul-Salaam, Palmer-Brown, Lobato

Sinovic	yellow card	4'
Blessing	goal	25'
Salloi	goal	66'
Opara	yellow card	90+6'
Long	yellow card	27'
Adams	yellow card	57'
Wright-Phillips	goal	90+1'

PRIMARY KIT 1996

PRIMARY KIT 2021

CREDITS THE SPORTING EXPERIENCE

166-167

The sun rises over One Sporting Way, the morning of the U.S. Open Cup Final, Sept. 20, 2017 (Nate Saathoff)

168-169

The façade of Children's Mercy Park prior to the gates opening, Sept. 29, 2019 (Simon Kuo); Turf Operations Manager Clayton Dame lays down chalk lines on the eve of a game (Mike Gunnoe); a corner flag is planted in the southwest corner of the stadium (Henry Hauck)

170-171

The players arrive: Gerso Fernandes and Roger Espinoza, March 4, 2018 (Olivia Brestal), and Daniel Salloi Aug. 10, 2019 (Henry Hauck); the boot room and locker room awaits their arrival, Sept. 9, 2016 (Nate Saathoff and Olivia Brestal)

172-173

Clockwise from left, Sporting players in warm-up lines before the match (Henry Hauck); Erik Hurtado, Matt Besler and Jimmy Medranda warm up in the hour before kickoff, Sept. 29, 2019 (Henry Hauck); Dom Dwyer stretches before a game (Henry Hauck); young fans get close to their favorite Sporting players, Sept. 8, 2018 (Henry Hauck)

174-175

The players walk out for the 2017 U.S. Open Cup Final, Sept. 20, 2017 (Gary Rohman); Matt Besler waits for the pregame coin toss vs. Atlanta, Aug. 6, 2017 (Gary Rohman); the SKC Starting XI engages in their customary pregame match photo hijinks, May 27, 2018 (Gary Rohman)

176-177

Graham Zusi, in a moment of quiet reflection before kickoff, Sept. 13, 2020 (Olivia Brestal); Dom Dwyer takes the field, Sept. 9, 2016 (Henry Hauck); Johnny Russell exhorts his teammates in the final seconds before kickoff, Nov. 22, 2020 (Olivia Brestal)

178-179

"I believe that we will win!" Fans come from all over—young and old, Missouri and Kansas, friends and families, superstars and tiny tots—to take part in The Sporting Experience

180-181

Gerso Fernandes fires in a cross in a beam of light, June 23, 2018 (Mike Gunnoe); Tim Melia dives for a save, March 10, 2019 (Gary Rohman); Benny Feilhaber takes flight and fires home, July 29, 2017 (Mike Gunnoe)

182-183

The celebration in the Cauldron begins, April 5, 2013 (Mike Gunnoe); Dom Dwyer does his patented post-goal flip, April 9, 2017 (Mike Gunnoe); confetti rains down after a goal in the Western Conference quarterfinal, Nov. 14, 2018 (Henry Hauck); the sky is blue with celebratory smoke, May 20, 2015

184-185

The postmatch victory sway after a Concacaf Champions League win over Toluca, Feb. 22, 2019 (Olivia Brestal)

186-187

Benny Feilhaber claps for the fans, May 18, 2019 (Henry Hauck); Tim Melia offers his jersey to a young fan, April 9, 2017 (Mike Gunnoe); Ilie Sanchez autographs a jersey after a win, Aug. 17, 2019 (Henry Hauck)

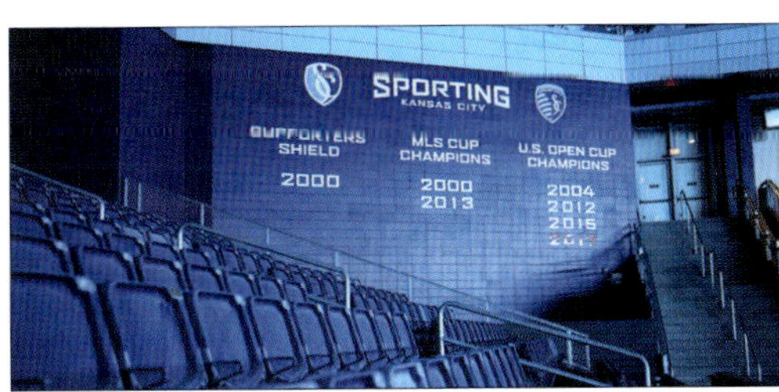

188-189

The sun sets on a work in progress, with more wall painting to follow, November 11, 2018 (Olivia Brestal)

CREDITS

CONTRIBUTORS

Carter Augustine ("My Story" series collaborator) has enjoyed nearly a decade at Sporting and thinks there's nothing quite like a big night at Children's Mercy Park.

Kurt Austin ("Growing Pains"), a coollector of soccer books, serves as Sporting KC's Director of Communications and has worked for the club for 11 seasons.

Dave Borchardt ("My Story" series collaborator) has spent his career in the Kansas City sports scene, having worked for Sports Radio 810 WHB, the Kansas City Wizards/Sporting KC and the Kansas City Sports Commission; He hosts Sporting KC's "The Final Whistle" postmatch radio show.

Mike Gunnoe ("Snapshots") is a Kansas City-based photographer who specializes in sports and editorial photography. Currently Mike is a contracted photographer for the Univerity of Kansas Athletics and Sporting Kansas City.

Josh Hakala ("Lamar's Trophy") has been a broadcast journalist/play-by-play announcer for more than 20 years, as well as creator/senior editor of TheCup.us, the premier source of U.S. Open Cup coverage past and present.

Sam Kovzan ("Wizards at Work," "Starting Over"), a lifelong fan, has worked in the club's communications department since graduating from the University of Kansas in 2014.

Michael MacCambridge (Editor) grew up in Kansas City and has written several books, including *America's Game: The Epic Story of How Pro Football Captured A Nation.*

Cortney Park (Lead Designer), a Kansas City native, grew up in a sports-loving family but never watched soccer; Since joining the club five seasons ago she is now a soccer convert and thinks it might be her favorite sport.

Laura Pfeifauf (Copyeditor/Proofreader) has been wordsmithing for 23 years, first for a large marketing agency and currently for a tech company in Kansas City, and loves being called a grammar ninja.

Sam Pierron ("No Other Club") was the first president of The Mystics, chairman of the original Supporters' Shield project, and president of the Heart of America Soccer Foundation; he is currently an IT consultant.

Chad Reynolds (Editor, "No Surrender," "Starting Over,") attended his first Wiz match in 1996 at age 12 and joined the front office in 2006; since 2015 he has been Sporting's Creative Director; He co-hosts Sporting KC's "The Final Whistle" postmatch radio show.

Nate Saathoff (Designer)—a corn-fed Iowan and a big fan of fountains—has been with Sporting KC for 6 seasons and loves Ilie hugs.

PHOTO CREDITS

Andy Mead: 29, 59; Angie Walton: 111; Aubrey Washington: 197; Brace Hemmelgarn: 192; Brett Davis: 109; Brian Davidson: 131; Denny Medley: 114, 123, 191, 192, 196; Doug Pensigner: 45; Ed Zurga: 6-7, 39, 40, 43; Elliott Pepich: 165; Elsa: 193; Eric Schlueter: 61, 78; Ezra Shaw: 194; G. Newman Lowrance: 52, 57, 80, 193; Gary Rohman: 151, 192; Henry Hauck: 133, 161, 165; Jacquelyn Martin: 119; Jay Biggerstaff: 193; Jeff Gross: 38, 138, 194; Joe Nicholson: 141; John Rieger: 108, 112, 113; Johnny Nunez: 118; Kelvin Kuo: 194; Madi Winfield: 103; Matt "Soda" Potter: 63, 67, 94, 95; Matthew Stockman: 48; Mike Gunnoe: 106, 118, 164; Mike Stobe: 197; Nate Saathoff: 103, 163; Nick Tre Smith: 133; Olivia Brestal: 100, 120, 128, 134, 158, 192; Peter Aiken: 111, 122, 160, 191, 194, 195, 196, 197; Rick Bowmer: 110; Robert Laberge: 196; Scott Bales: 58; Scott Pribyl: 85, 86, 87; Simon Barnett: 30; Simon Kuo: 126; Stephen Dunn: 21, 22, 23, 26, 193, 196; Thad Bell: 159; Tim Umphrey: 4-5; Winslow Townson: 195; Zach Cobb: 8, 104, 115, 116, 117, 161, 162, 164, 165; MLS Archives: 18; SKC Archives: 2-3, 24, 25, 34, 36, 41, 42, 44, 47, 54, 64, 96, 130, 132, 191, 195; Courtesy of Populous: 89; Courtesy of Mike Gaughan: 152, 154; Courtesy of Mike Kuhn: 153; Courtesy of Andy Mead: 155; Courtesy of Derek Gathright: 157

SPORTING ASSOCIATES

All of this would not be possible without our associates (at the time of printing):

Diego Acuna, David Adams, Kylie Adams, Blake Allee-Lightfoot, Gregg Allen, Kurt Andrews, Chioma Atanmo, Carter Augustine, Kurt Austin, Nick Barbalato, Chris Beck, Cole Befort, Chris Behrens, Patrik Bergabo, Josh Blackford, David Blakesley, Brian Bliss, Martin Bolanos, Lakyn Boltz, Jordan Borel, Aaron Borns, Chris Boyajian, Meghan Cameron, Jason Cannito, Colby Childress, Courtney Claassen, Selena Corpuz, Ronald Culver, Caleb Dachtler, Clayton Dame, Olivia Diehl, Alan Dietrich, Devan Dignan, Josh Duffy, Alec Dufty, Maggie Duggan, Thomas Earle, Katie Eichman, Greg Esenberg, Andrew Faerber, Jon Farrell, Jackie Feeney, Benny Feilhaber, Colby Fell, Derek Ferguson, Jordan Fitzpatrick, Mike Flaherty, Jillian Foster, Matthew Fucaloro, Drew Fuemmeler, Connor Galloway, Andy Garay-Moreno, Matt Gerstner, Stacy Gewecke, Isaac Gomez, Alec Graves, James Gregoire, Nic Guess, Sami Hameid, Heather Handwork, Caleb Hargarten, Joey Harty, Matt Hefley, Sarah Hooper, Jordan Hummel, Nathan Hunt, Sam Jaksen, Boomer Jenkins, Declan Jogi, Khalid Jones, Ryan Kaufman, Jordan Kelsey, Andrea Kimball, Andrew King, Matt Knight, Ashley Koehn, Sam Kovzan, Wan Kuzac, Rachel Lammers, Brenna Lane, Sam Lane, Joe Lanning, Kevin Lawson, Randi Lininger, Andy Lockard, Sergio Loeza, Dwyane Lovingood, Nolan MacGregor, Darrin MacLeod, Justin Madsen, Chris Martinez, Sonny Martinez, Abe Mathew, Garrett Maxey, Betsy Maxfield, Tyler McBee, Meesh McDaniel, Blake McFarland, John Moncke, Casey Montgomery, Jon Moses, Aaron Mull, Nick Mullen, Rumbani Munthali, Alexis Myers, Paulo Nagamura, Erin Nelson, Chet North, Chris O'Neal, Sheri Osborn, Luis Pacheco, Cortney Park, Jon Parry, Will Patterson, Alex Peters, Ashley Pettigrew, Stewart Pirani, Paulo Pita, Dan Popik, Jake Reid, Chad Reynolds, Anthony Rios, Joseph Robertson, Scott Robinette, Diane Robison, Nikki Romolo, Kyleigh Rowe, Nate Saathoff, Nick Sambol, Tony Sambol, Alejandro Sanchez, Zoran Savic, Weston Schroeder, Laine Schwarberg, Eric Schwartz, Kristi Simmons, Alec Smith, Chris Smith, Joshua Smith, Kellen Smith, Tammy Stauffer, Michael Steidle, Jared Stilger, Kristen Stivers, Wilson Temple, Alphonso Thompson, Derek Thompson, Rob Thomson, Jared Turk, Peter Vermes, Erin Vierzba, Jeff Vogel, Ashley Wallace, Jamie Washington, Ryan Wells, Becca Wheaton, Brennan Williams, Brennan Wingert, Chris Wolbert, Kerry Zavagnin, Brooke Zimmerman

ACKNOWLEDGMENTS

It starts with an idea.

And in this case, the idea came during an early discussion, in the spring of 2020, among Sporting Kansas City's client services and marketing associates, about gift ideas for the annual season-ticket member mailing for 2021. Traditionally, these gift boxes have included tickets, as well as other assorted souvenirs for supporters. When the club switched to a mobile ticketing process in 2017, a renewed emphasis emerged on finding just the right gift to season-ticket members.

"How about a really nice coffee-table book?" suggested Creative Services Manager and Designer Cortney Park.

And with that, the process began. A book is a general idea. What kind of book was the telling detail, and in this, the group soon settled on 2021 being an ideal year to celebrate and document the first 25 years of Major League Soccer in Kansas City. The organizing principle was to tell the remarkable story of the club's evolution, showing both the highlights and the missteps along the way, and take the measure of the distance traveled—in a way that would be cherished and appreciated by season-ticket members and compelling for those who have more recently grown attached to the club and "The Sporting Experience."

With Creative Director Chad Reynolds overseeing the editorial portion of the book and Park taking the lead on the design, I was brought in as a hired gun to help coordinate the editorial effort.

No one spent more time on this book than the indefatigable Reynolds, who in addition to writing two key pieces about the club's evolution, also possessed the granular institutional memory to be able to look at a picture and tell at a glance, "That was from the 2011 Western Conference semifinal, because that was the signage we were using back then."

In addition to overseeing the majority of the design elements, Park conceived and executed the Wizards and Sporting timelines, chronicling the club's history in a way that is at once graphically striking and richly informative. Nate Saathoff provided graphic design support with the club's kit history and the "XXV for 25" feature.

In telling the story of this club's epic journey, there is no substitute for the participants and witnesses who lived through it. To that end, the twelve present and former Wizards and Sporting greats shared their stories, aided by the insightful questions of Dave Borchardt and Carter Augustine. Sam Kovzan drew rich, intimate portraits of the title seasons of 2000 and 2013; Kurt Austin pieced together the humble early days of the club; Josh Hakala weighed in on the rich history of the Lamar Hunt U.S. Open Cup; Sam Pierron compiled the epic oral history of the club's supporters' culture. Laura Pfeifauf, a longtime supporter in her own right, came on to handle the copy-editing and proofreading and the marshaling of stray Oxford commas.

With this endeavor, as with all the things Sporting, we owe a major debt of gratitude for the guidance and support provided by the club's visionary ownership group: the Patterson, Illig, Curran, Maday and Heineman families. At critical junctures in the process, Jake Reid, Rob Thomson and Aaron Borns provided oversight and guidance.

The brilliant photography featured in the book comes from Olivia Brestal, Mike Gunnoe, Gary Rohman, Henry Hauck, Zach Cobb, Nate Saathoff, Andy Mead and Matt "Soda" Potter, among others. In telling the story, we drew from Sporting KC archives and many of the collections of those working with the club, as well as Robert Houghton, Chris Wyche, Mike Kuhn, Mike Gaughan and Jon Adams. We also appreciate the contributions of MLS Commisioner Don Garber and Dan Courtemanche at the league office.

Special thanks to editorial matchmaker Jean Lucas and longtime supporter Greg Emas for early thoughts on the process. Thanks as well for crucial assistance in the latter stages from Todd and Anissa Everett, Kiran and Harika Nagarajan, Trey Gratwick, Ella MacCambridge, Miles MacCambridge and Rob Minter. Special thanks as well to Bob Audley of the Covington Group Kansas City.

A quarter-century went by fast. This is a celebration of not only what has been built along the way, but also for what has been received. Of a club becoming part of a city, and a city—on both sides of the state line—that has truly become a part of this club.

—MM, Austin, March 2021